EIGHTH DAY PRAYERS

DAILY HOPE *FOR* ADVENT,
CHRISTMAS, *AND* EPIPHANY

Sally Breedlove, Willa Kane,
Madison Perry, and Alysia Yates

Forefront
BOOKS

Eighth Day Prayers: Daily Hope for Advent, Christmas, and Epiphany

By Sally Breedlove, Willa Kane, Madison Perry, and Alysia Yates.

Cover image & Eighth Day emblem design: Isabel Yates

Library of Congress Control Number: 2024905953

ISBN: 978-1-63763-314-4
E-book ISBN: 978-1-63763-315-1

Published by Forefront Books, Nashville, Tennessee.

Distributed by Simon & Schuster.

Cover Design: Jonathan Lewis
Interior Design by Bill Kersey, KerseyGraphics

Dedication

For Lekita Essa, widowed young, who turned grief into
a way to love others. She heard the Holy Spirit's call
to prayer and shared it with an anxious world.

And for Beatrice Rose Dasher, whose brief eighty-
eight days helped those who knew her steadfast peace
learn to hope in the resurrection of the body
and the life of the world to come.

Contents

Introduction

MADISON PERRY

*W*HAT DAY IS IT? No matter the week or season, there is another name for the day you are living: the eighth day. Jesus Christ was resurrected the day after the last day of the week. If the first day was a day of creation, the eighth day was one of new creation and life in Christ on the far side of the grave. By the power of the Holy Spirit, you can join Christ and live in this new day, even in the midst of the old order.

This book is an invitation to live like eighth-day people. You are invited to a banquet, to feast in the halls of Zion and dwell forever in the kingdom of God. At this table lies nothing less than everything, no matter what you have lost or suffered, or even what you have inflicted on the world around you.

This invitation is present on every page of the Bible. However, left to our own devices, we do not have eyes to see God's glory or ears to hear God's call. Adrift in the imagination of our hearts, we wander through the ruins of another age.

How do we enter this realm of God's resurrection glory? By the work of the Holy Spirit through God's Word. His Word is living and active, capable of piercing even to the dividing of soul and spirit, and his mercies are new every morning.

You likely recognize that you are in the same decaying world that we all experience, where our sense of history comes from the news cycle and to-do lists. This is the stale kingdom of the age that is passing away. What will quicken our hearts, rebuild our imaginations, and pull us back toward our God on a daily basis? Surely God's Word is up to the challenge.

Within *Eighth Day Prayers* you will find passages of Scripture that pull you into the world of God's Word, new landscapes of fresh truth where the Holy Spirit will equip you for friendship with God. We hope that this book moves you to engage with Scripture and that our words will recede, leaving you open to God's Word and its power. We cannot set the terms of your engagement with God, but we hope to guide you into what may feel like new terrain and prepare you for real life—life with Christ.

We have ordered *Eighth Day Prayers* to follow the church's calendar, and the newly revised format is comprised of three volumes: the Incarnation Cycle contains Advent, Christmas, and Epiphany; the Paschal Cycle contains Lent, Holy Week, Easter, and Pentecost; and the final volume contains Ordinary Time. Each season begins with a brief introduction, and we have added a calendar at the beginning of each page for your convenience. Following the church's calendar will give you the opportunity to connect your daily exposure to God's Word with the expansive story of God's redeeming work. Here we find an older, truer way of living, one that draws its momentum from the arc of salvation and discovers deep wells of rest and strength in Christ.

As you immerse yourself in the Word of God, open yourself to his Spirit, and orient yourself within the life of Jesus, we pray that you will move into a new and richer reality. The kingdom of God is near. Repent, believe, and find your life in the gospel!

Entering In
STEPHEN A. MACCHIA

*T*HE BEST PART OF CONVERSATIONS with new friends is the give-and-take: We don't already know what they are going to say. We notice things about them that we enjoy even as we converse. We are curious, we ask questions, we share real things. We listen hard because the person matters to us. They are not a book we have already read; they are not present merely to tell us what to do or what is wrong with us. They want to know us, and we want to know them.

The ancient practice of *lectio* is like that—it's listening to God's Word, listening to what arises in our hearts as we hear God's Word, and responding in prayer to the Author of these words with real words of our own. *Lectio* is conversation between the triune God and us, the children he so deeply loves, in the context of his beautiful Word.

Consider these ancient words used to describe this way of being with God during *lectio*:

- We pause for silence and still our hearts to receive God's Word (*silencio*).
- We receive a sacred reading of the text (*lectio*).
- We notice a particular word or image that has leapt off the page into our hearts, and we meditate on that word or image (*meditatio*).
- We prayerfully respond to what we notice stirring in our own heart (*oratio*).
- We linger in silence, noticing more deeply how this particular Scripture is speaking to us (*contemplatio*).
- We say yes to the transforming work God is seeking to do in us as we hold this word from him. How is our soul being nourished and transformed? How are we being called to be and to do in our life in this world (*incarnatio*)?

In many ways this book is designed to guide you into a time of *lectio* so you can focus on a small portion of God's Word and enter into a prayerful encounter with the living God. When Bible reading becomes prayer, you know you've touched a nerve the Spirit is inviting you to consider. There is a fresh wind of God's Spirit when we genuinely receive the living Word, and it is profoundly good for our souls.

You are blessed to be holding this resource in your hands. May the words of your mouth and the meditations of your heart be inspired by the Word and then multiplied in your soul and in service to others. Receive what God has in store for you like you've never heard the Word before.

Such joy!

Introduction to the Christian Year
STEVEN E. BREEDLOVE

FROM THE MOMENT GOD CREATED THE WORLD, he rooted it in time. The six days of creation are endowed with beauty, meaning, and purpose, leading us to the seventh day of divine rest. But what of the eighth day? For Christians the eighth day is the day of Jesus's resurrection from the dead—Easter—on the first day after the Jewish Sabbath. The eighth day marks a new way of keeping time shaped by the inbreaking of a new creation.

Time tells a story. And the way we tell time inscribes that story in us. As Christians we are eighth-day people, thus the inspiration for eight-sided churches, pulpits, stained glass windows, and the emblem that adorns the cover and pages of this book. We have titled this book *Eighth Day Prayers* as an invitation to a new way of keeping time, one rooted in the rhythm of creation that nonetheless draws us on toward new creation.

In so many ways we have lost our ability to keep time. Perhaps this loss results from the movement away from an agricultural world, where land was left fallow for a season before it was sown and where sowing necessarily preceded growing, which resulted in harvest. It was impossible in the agricultural world to divorce one season from another, and each season contributed its own gift and preparation to the next. But this loss of connection between the seasons is also the result of trading the church calendar for the economic calendar, where every season is harvest and none is planting.

The church calendar is not a series of discrete seasons, yet the tyranny of the economic calendar makes it initially difficult to see this. Throughout the centuries, the church has recognized that the Christian year consists of two cycles. In other words, we don't have Advent, Christmas, and Epiphany. Instead, we have the Incarnation Cycle, which consists of Advent, Christmas, and Epiphany. And we don't have Lent, Easter, and Pentecost. Instead, we have the Paschal Cycle, which consists of Lent, Easter, and Pentecost. In each of these cycles, the seasons are intricately connected to and dependent on one another, and in each, the pattern is the same—preparation, celebration, and growth.

In a previous age, we might have simply said that mortification and repentance must precede rejoicing, because they sow the seeds for it, and that rejoicing is the foundation for growth, discipleship, and mission, because we reap a harvest from the object of our rejoicing. We cannot divorce Lent from Easter, and we cannot divorce Easter from Pentecost.

Each season prepares for the next, and trying to live the spiritual life in only one season is like trying to have only harvest without sowing. We need to be planted anew each year. The Christian year offers us the framework for this.

As you let *Eighth Day Prayers* help shape your day-by-day prayers, notice how your response to Scripture and your prayers change as you hold in mind what season it is. Is it a time for preparation? For rejoicing? For a rekindled awareness of God's presence and his call to us?

God himself has given us the gift of agricultural seasons and the gift of the rhythm of the Christian year. Let them draw you more deeply into a prayer-filled life with God.

Introduction to Advent
STEVEN E. BREEDLOVE

*A*DVENT IS A SEASON OF HOPEFUL WAITING for the coming of Christ.

We fast in Advent, but it is a fast motivated by expectation, not penitence. It is like anticipating a wedding banquet, which we would hardly prepare for by eating too much cheap food. Instead, we wait with modest fasting, with joy and expectation, because a rich and lavish feast is coming. The certainty of Christmas offers us the ability to wait patiently and steadfastly.

It is ultimately the return of Christ, not Christmas, that we await in Advent. The first coming is proof that the second will also arrive, and our joyful waiting for Christmas should prepare us for Christ's return. More than anything, this is the season of the year when we should cultivate longing and hope for the second coming of Christ.

Prayer in Advent is marked by this expectation and grounded in the truth that Christ will come again and restore all things. Every reading of Scripture should be considered from the standpoint, "What will this mean when Christ returns?" The season offers us a particular form of discipleship— training in expectancy as we wait within the tension of Christ's first and second coming. It is the season when, even as we learn hopeful patience, our hearts resound with the prayer, *Lord, I long for your return! Please prepare me to celebrate your arrival!*

Advent Day 1
WILLA KANE

Read: *Isaiah 48:12–17*

"Listen to me, O Jacob,
    and Israel, whom I called!
I am he; I am the first,
    and I am the last.
My hand laid the foundation of the earth,
    and my right hand spread out the heavens;
when I call to them,
    they stand forth together.
"Assemble, all of you, and listen!
    Who among them has declared these things?
The LORD loves him;
        he shall perform his purpose on Babylon,
        and his arm shall be against the Chaldeans.
I, even I, have spoken and called him;
        I have brought him, and he will prosper in his way.
Draw near to me, hear this:
        from the beginning I have not spoken in secret,
        from the time it came to be I have been there."
And now the LORD God has sent me, and his Spirit.
Thus says the LORD,
        your Redeemer, the Holy One of Israel:
"I am the LORD your God,
        who teaches you to profit,
        who leads you in the way you should go."

Reflect:

Advent is a journey of preparation. The prophet Isaiah invited us to this journey at the behest of someone greater than himself: the I Am, the first and the last, the Creator God whose hand laid the foundation of the earth and spread out the heavens. God does not speak in secret or stand at a distance. He has been present from the beginning of time.

14

Two hundred years before Babylon took Israel captive, God spoke these words through Isaiah. Persia's King Cyrus would be chosen, called, and prospered by God to release Jewish captives from Babylon for return to Zion, fulfilling God's purpose. Two thousand years before our day, God sent another, greater one to redeem his people. This Redeemer would come not as a conquering hero but as an infant King. The birth of Jesus in a Bethlehem stable under a starlit sky is the place where prophecy and promise come together.

This Advent journey's destination is not to a place but to a person we are invited to know. What will you do with this invitation? As you pray, will you slow your pace and listen? Will you examine and empty your heart of things that crowd the Savior out, preparing your heart by preparing him room? Will you come near to the one who has come near to you? He leads in the way you should go, one step of the journey at a time. Will you follow him?

And as you do, will you focus beyond this horizon to a second advent, to a day when Jesus will come again to redeem his people and begin a glorious eternity? Just as he created earth's foundations and stretched out the heavens, he will do so again. In re-creation glory he will bring forth the new heaven and earth, our eternal home.

Pray:

Almighty God, give us grace to cast away the works of darkness, and put on the armor of light, now in the time of this mortal life in which your Son Jesus Christ came to visit us in great humility; that in the last day, when he shall come again in his glorious majesty to judge both the living and the dead, we may rise to the life immortal; through him who lives and reigns with you and the Holy Spirit, one God, now and forever. Amen.

(Anglican Church in North America Book of Common Prayer)

Advent Day 2
ART GOING

Read: *Isaiah 49:1–6*

> Listen to me, O coastlands,
>> and give attention, you peoples from afar.
> The LORD called me from the womb,
>> from the body of my mother he named my name.
> He made my mouth like a sharp sword;
>> in the shadow of his hand he hid me;
> he made me a polished arrow;
>> in his quiver he hid me away.
> And he said to me, "You are my servant,
>> Israel, in whom I will be glorified."
> But I said, "I have labored in vain;
>> I have spent my strength for nothing and vanity;
> yet surely my right is with the LORD,
>> and my recompense with my God."
> And now the LORD says,
>> he who formed me from the womb to be his servant,
> to bring Jacob back to him;
>> and that Israel might be gathered to him—
> for I am honored in the eyes of the LORD,
>> and my God has become my strength—
> he says:
> "It is too light a thing that you should be my servant
>> to raise up the tribes of Jacob
>> and to bring back the preserved of Israel;
> I will make you as a light for the nations,
>> that my salvation may reach to the end of the earth."

Reflect:

Isaiah 49 is the second of the towering servant songs of Isaiah. There at the beginning is that Advent word: *listen!*

The promise of the Servant's coming is not for captive Israel only.

16

God's Servant will be "a light for the nations." God's salvation is going global!

In the face of uncertainty and polarization, at the beginning of a possibly dark winter season, is there light for the nations? Is there a message of hope?

This passage in Isaiah gives us a resounding yes! We will have a new beginning and an everlasting Savior. We will see salvation stretching to the ends of the earth. There is no better news for our weary world.

Isaiah beckons us to let God have the last word and to listen to his promise. He will reconnect his people with himself and put the world in order.

As you pray, are you able to imagine yourself being called to be a part of God's servant people, the ones he will use to bring light to the nations? As you hear that promise, pray for God to kindle in you a holy imagination, and ask how you might be a light-bringer this season.

Pray:

Lighten our darkness, we beseech you, O Lord; and by your great mercy defend us from all perils and dangers of this night; for the love of your only Son, our Savior Jesus Christ. Amen.

(Anglican Church in North America Book of Common Prayer)

Advent Day 3
ART GOING

Read: *Isaiah 50:4–5, 10*

> The Lord GOD has given me
>> the tongue of those who are taught,
> that I may know how to sustain with a word
>> him who is weary.
> Morning by morning he awakens;
>> he awakens my ear
>> to hear as those who are taught.
> The Lord GOD has opened my ear,
>> and I was not rebellious;
>> I turned not backward....
> Who among you fears the LORD
>> and obeys the voice of his servant?
> Let him who walks in darkness
>> and has no light
> trust in the name of the LORD
>> and rely on his God.

Reflect:

Does God waken your ear to hear? Does the Lord speak to you through his Word? The prophet's vivid imagery describes an everyday experience of listening in anticipation of hearing a word. Of course, Isaiah 50—before it was a word to and about us—was first a picture of Jesus, the Servant. Can you picture the Lord beginning each day having his ear opened to hear as those who are taught? Jesus's decisive response was obedience rooted in listening.

We also read so that we may hear as obedient servants. We hear so that we may be comforters. Our Comforter bids us back each day for a fresh word. Isaiah 50 invites us into this rhythmic vocation.

The driving impulse for our listening is so that we will know how to sustain with a word someone who is weary. You likely won't have to look far to find a weary friend or family member. Do you have a word for them?

As you pray, remember that everything depends on your becoming a hearer before God. Take time each day—at best, a regular fixed time—to read the Bible and to listen quietly for a word spoken to you. Ask for your heart to be stirred for a living conversation with the Father in prayer. And ask for a word that you may share with someone in need.

Pray:

Blessed Lord, who caused all Holy Scriptures to be written for our learning: Grant us so to hear them, read, mark, learn, and inwardly digest them, that by patience and the comfort of your holy Word we may embrace and ever hold fast the blessed hope of everlasting life, which you have given us in our Savior Jesus Christ; who lives and reigns with you and the Holy Spirit, one God, for ever and ever. Amen.

(Anglican Church in North America Book of Common Prayer)

Advent Day 4
ART GOING

Read: *Isaiah 51:1–5, 7*

> "Listen to me, you who pursue righteousness,
>> you who seek the LORD:
> look to the rock from which you were hewn,
>> and to the quarry from which you were dug.
> Look to Abraham your father
>> and to Sarah who bore you;
> for he was but one when I called him,
>> that I might bless him and multiply him.
> For the LORD comforts Zion;
>> he comforts all her waste places
> and makes her wilderness like Eden,
>> her desert like the garden of the LORD;
> joy and gladness will be found in her,
>> thanksgiving and the voice of song.
> "Give attention to me, my people,
>> and give ear to me, my nation;
> for a law will go out from me,
>> and I will set my justice for a light to the peoples.
> My righteousness draws near,
>> my salvation has gone out,
>> and my arms will judge the peoples;
> the coastlands hope for me,
>> and for my arm they wait....
> "Listen to me, you who know righteousness,
>> the people in whose heart is my law;
> fear not the reproach of man,
>> nor be dismayed at their revilings."

Reflect:

Throughout Advent, God desires to keep us in an attentive frame of mind. "Ponder the rock from which you were cut," reads another version of Isaiah

51:1 (MSG). The Lord invites you to ponder, to look back, and to reflect on *the rock from which you were hewn*. Look back to Abraham and the call to go out, not knowing anything except God's promise and assured companionship. That's one of the fruits of listening and pondering; we get reacquainted with the Promise-Giver, and he transforms our perspective.

Isaiah 51 is packed with incentives to keep listening to God. The first incentive is that God is a life-giver. If he could bless old Abraham and barren Sarah with new life, and out of that unlikely beginning create a nation to bless the nations, then why wouldn't he do something new with you and me? What blessing and multiplication can you imagine in your life?

Not only that, but God is also a world-changer. Do you like the way the world is now? Neither does God. The difference between you and him is that he can change it—through his life-transforming gospel. Maybe it's time to turn off the news of the day and tune in to the good news of God's redeeming work.

Finally, our God is a courage-inspirer. Don't be afraid. He made you. He will be your Comforter, your Keeper, your Friend.

As you pray, think about Abraham and Sarah, and celebrate that you were hewn from the same rock. Pray with hopeful anticipation of God's unremitting new creation. The apostle Paul loved reminding his fellow believers that God had promised to send the Holy Spirit, who would *come alongside to build them up*. Pray for that!

Pray:

O, Father, fill our hearts with faith. Come alongside us, Holy Spirit, and lead us in the way everlasting. Be our Comforter, our Keeper, our Friend. In the precious name of Jesus. Amen.

Advent Day 5
ART GOING

Read: *Isaiah 52:7–10*

> How beautiful upon the mountains
> > are the feet of him who brings good news,
>
> who publishes peace, who brings good news of happiness,
> > who publishes salvation,
> > who says to Zion, "Your God reigns."
>
> The voice of your watchmen—they lift up their voice;
> > together they sing for joy;
>
> for eye to eye they see
> > the return of the LORD to Zion.
>
> Break forth together into singing,
> > you waste places of Jerusalem,
>
> for the LORD has comforted his people;
> > he has redeemed Jerusalem.
>
> The LORD has bared his holy arm
> > before the eyes of all the nations,
>
> and all the ends of the earth shall see
> > the salvation of our God.

Reflect:

Can you hear it? In the din of our noisy world, through the relentless voices inside our heads, amid the onslaught of social media, can you hear the steps of the runner?

Who is racing into your life these days to bring good news? Who are the messengers announcing to you and reminding you that "your God reigns"?

It's easy to lose sight of God's reign in the commotion of our lives.

Where are you hearing a counter-message of sovereign order and a promise of flourishing?

Whose voice is cutting through the noise to incite your hope? Are you paying attention to the God-appointed promise-bringers? And are you giving thanks for those who are working nimbly and tirelessly to penetrate the cacophony of despair?

Maybe these days you're feeling the nudge of the Spirit to strap on your gospel shoes and to proclaim God's peace. Maybe he is calling you to bring good news—the good news of Jesus—to fearful and discouraged family, friends, and neighbors. Maybe you are called to build up those around you by speaking these beautiful and true things about God.

Wouldn't that be a delightful focus as you pray?

Invite the Holy Spirit to come alongside you and encourage you to be a road-racing messenger of good news. And keep praying for all the messengers out there: "How beautiful . . . are the feet of those who bring good news" (Isaiah 52:7 NIV).

Pray:

Almighty God, you sent your Son Jesus Christ to reconcile the world to yourself: We praise and bless you for those whom you have sent in the power of the Spirit to preach the Gospel to all nations. We thank you that in all parts of the earth a community of love has been gathered together by their prayers and labors, and that in every place your servants call upon your Name; for the kingdom and the power and the glory are yours, for ever and ever. Amen.

(Anglican Church in North America Book of Common Prayer)

Advent Day 6
ART GOING

Read: *Isaiah 53:3–6*

> He was despised and rejected by men,
>> a man of sorrows and acquainted with grief;
> and as one from whom men hide their faces
>> he was despised, and we esteemed him not.
> Surely he has borne our griefs
>> and carried our sorrows;
> yet we esteemed him stricken,
>> smitten by God, and afflicted.
> But he was pierced for our transgressions;
>> he was crushed for our iniquities;
> upon him was the chastisement that brought us peace,
>> and with his wounds we are healed.
> All we like sheep have gone astray;
>> we have turned—every one—to his own way;
> and the LORD has laid on him
>> the iniquity of us all.

Reflect:

Many of us have a hard time with silence and solitude and the thoughts that surface in those moments. We don't always like what comes to mind when we lie awake in the quiet of the night.

It's hard to silence the accusing internal voice as we're pressed into self-appraisal. How to still those thoughts? What will make the unbearable guilt and shame go away? Who can bear it for us? Do we have to just live with it?

The season of Advent restarts the wondrous cycle of the church's year of redemption; it begins afresh the story of our coming King. Isaiah 53 reminds us that we need to hear and meet again and again, not just the baby in the manger but also the sin-bearer, Jesus—our substitute.

As you reflect on Isaiah 53, trace the life-giving progression of our guilt being met by Christ, our substitute, who counters our shame with his healing grace. The cycle begins with our owning who we are. "If we say we have no sin, we deceive ourselves, and the truth is not in us. If we confess our sins, he is faithful and just to forgive us our sins and to cleanse us from all unrighteousness" (1 John 1:8–9).

As you pray, pray your way slowly into this ancient prayer of confession, and give thanks that you get to live in the life-giving rhythm of grace.

Pray:

Almighty God, Father of our Lord Jesus Christ, maker and judge of us all: We acknowledge and lament our many sins and offenses, which we have committed by thought, word, and deed against your divine majesty, provoking most justly your righteous anger against us. We are deeply sorry for these our transgressions; the burden of them is more than we can bear. Have mercy upon us, Have mercy upon us, most merciful Father for your Son our Lord Jesus Christ's sake, forgive us all that is past; and grant that we may evermore serve and please you in newness of life, to the honor and glory of your Name; through Jesus Christ our Lord. Amen.

(Anglican Church in North America Book of Common Prayer)

Advent Day 7
ART GOING

Read: *Isaiah 54:1–6, 10*

"Sing, O barren one, who did not bear;
  break forth into singing and cry aloud,
  you who have not been in labor!
For the children of the desolate one will be more
  than the children of her who is married," says the LORD.
"Enlarge the place of your tent,
  and let the curtains of your habitations be stretched out;
do not hold back; lengthen your cords
  and strengthen your stakes.
For you will spread abroad to the right and to the left,
  and your offspring will possess the nations
  and will people the desolate cities.
"Fear not, for you will not be ashamed;
  be not confounded, for you will not be disgraced;
for you will forget the shame of your youth,
  and the reproach of your widowhood you will remember
  no more.
For your Maker is your husband,
  the LORD of hosts is his name;
and the Holy One of Israel is your Redeemer,
  the God of the whole earth he is called.
For the LORD has called you
  like a wife deserted and grieved in spirit,
like a wife of youth when she is cast off,
  says your God....
"For the mountains may depart
  and the hills be removed,
but my steadfast love shall not depart from you, and my covenant of peace shall not be removed," says the LORD, who has
  compassion on you.

Reflect:

Isaiah took a long, loving look at the sin-bearing servant of the Lord and had one thing to say: "Sing."

Perhaps singing is a hard prospect for you. Perhaps life feels too arduous or painful, and singing is the last activity you want to engage in.

But there is that urgent appeal in Isaiah 54:1: "Sing, O barren one, who did not bear; break forth into singing and cry aloud, you who have not been in labor!"

Let joyful song explode out of you—you who see your emptiness filled, your wilderness blooming!

As we've been listening to Isaiah, and through him to the Lord, we've been called again and again to remember God's mercy, to be refreshed by his promises, to have our hope rekindled, and to be sent forth as messengers ourselves, fueled by the Spirit of the God who loves. And now we're urged to sing!

The people of God sang. Moses sang. Miriam sang. Deborah sang. David sang. Mary sang. Angels sang. Jesus and his disciples sang. Paul and Silas sang. When people of faith remember who God is and what God does, they sing. The songs are irrepressible.

Singing is an expression of defiant joy in the face of overwhelming sadness. Suffer we do, but sing we must!

As you pray, why not let your voice sound forth? Sing!

Pray:

Oh sing to the LORD a new song; sing to the LORD, all the earth! Sing to the LORD, bless his name; tell of his salvation from day to day. Declare his glory among the nations, his marvelous works among all the peoples! For great is the LORD, and greatly to be praised. Amen.

(Psalm 96:1–4)

Advent Day 8

TAMARA HILL MURPHY

Read: *Isaiah 55:1–3, 7–9, 12*

"Come, everyone who thirsts,
      come to the waters;
and he who has no money,
      come, buy and eat!
Come, buy wine and milk
      without money and without price.
Why do you spend your money for that which is not bread,
      and your labor for that which does not satisfy?
Listen diligently to me, and eat what is good,
      and delight yourselves in rich food.
Incline your ear, and come to me;
      hear, that your soul may live;
and I will make with you an everlasting covenant,
      my steadfast, sure love for David....
"Let the wicked forsake his way,
      and the unrighteous man his thoughts;
let him return to the LORD, that he may have compassion on him,
      and to our God, for he will abundantly pardon.
For my thoughts are not your thoughts,
      neither are your ways my ways, declares the LORD.
For as the heavens are higher than the earth,
      so are my ways higher than your ways
      and my thoughts than your thoughts....
"For you shall go out in joy
      and be led forth in peace;
the mountains and the hills before you
      shall break forth into singing,
      and all the trees of the field shall clap their hands."

Reflect:

Over and over again throughout Israel's history, we find that God's people can't discern between what satisfies and what destroys. The lack of discernment led them to give their most valuable offerings to idols and was rooted in a forgetfulness of all that came before them and all that was promised for the future. Having lost their taste for what truly satisfies, they could no longer imagine the pleasant land God had promised as something worth believing.

Nevertheless, God remembered his covenant. His wrath was consumed by his immense love, a love so contagious that it required even the Israelites' captors to show compassion for God's people. This love flows through the invitation in Isaiah 55. In contrast to the unmet cravings from living in an economy of idol worship, Yahweh summons everyone to come for the richest delights. He calls out like a street vendor offering the finest of all food and drink with no price.

This is God's economy. Humanity's habitual fascination with power continually sinks down into idolatrous practices filled with fear, anxiety, and scarcity. In the body and blood of his Son, Jesus, God overturns such a system.

As you come to pray, hear Christ's invitation from Luke 14:33: "So then, none of you can be My disciple who does not give up all his own possessions" (NASB). Jesus, the voice of Yahweh, picks up the cry of a holy street vendor. *Come, find a way of life that is free for everyone yet costs everything.*

Consider how responding to the call of Jesus brings the richest kind of delights found only in the free, gracious, and immense love of God. Give thanks to the Father, who will never forget his covenant and who will, in fact, bring all exiles home.

Pray:

Lord, just as our ancestors sinned and turned away from you, so have we also wandered. Forgive us, and welcome us back into the way of Jesus, so that we might delight in your abundant goodness and welcome others into the everlasting promise of your covenant. Amen.

Advent Day 9

TAMARA HILL MURPHY

Read: *Isaiah 56:3–8*

> Let not the foreigner who has joined himself to the LORD say,
>> "The LORD will surely separate me from his people";
> and let not the eunuch say,
>> "Behold, I am a dry tree."
> For thus says the LORD:
> "To the eunuchs who keep my Sabbaths,
>> who choose the things that please me
>> and hold fast my covenant,
> I will give in my house and within my walls
>> a monument and a name
>> better than sons and daughters;
> I will give them an everlasting name
>> that shall not be cut off.
> "And the foreigners who join themselves to the LORD,
>> to minister to him, to love the name of the LORD,
>> and to be his servants,
> everyone who keeps the Sabbath and does not profane it,
>> and holds fast my covenant—
> these I will bring to my holy mountain,
>> and make them joyful in my house of prayer;
> their burnt offerings and their sacrifices
>> will be accepted on my altar;
> for my house shall be called a house of prayer
>> for all peoples."
> The Lord GOD,
>> who gathers the outcasts of Israel, declares,
> "I will gather yet others to him
>> besides those already gathered."

Reflect:

Isaiah 55 assures us that Yahweh's economy is free yet costs everything; Isaiah 56 tells us who the beneficiaries of that economy are. Those who respond to the voice of Yahweh, spoken through Jesus, are invited in off the street to gather around the table. Everyone is welcome to the Lord's household.

Everyone is welcome, yet Yahweh reveals a certain zeal for the outcast. Not only the outcast in society's terms but also those who recognize within their own hearts that they are not worthy to be called sons and daughters. Yet they are so drawn to the household of God that they'd be willing to enter as mere servants of the one true King. To these few, God not only creates space within his household but also offers a "monument and a name better than sons and daughters" (v. 5). For those who do not presume through any human legitimacy to enter this economy except as servants to the just and righteous God, the Father makes a place of honor within his house.

It seems that Yahweh, the Creator of all humankind, cannot imagine a home without a place of honor for the outcast, the foreigner, and the prodigal. It has been said that to confront means to face a person coming toward you until you recognize him as a brother. The Father runs toward the outcast, seeing them as someone more highly valued than even a daughter or a son.

As you prepare to pray, ask God to increase your imagination about his house of prayer for all people. What does this look like? Where do you need to turn your gaze in order to be one who, like the Father, runs toward the outcast, the foreigner, and the prodigal?

Pray:

O God, you have made of one blood all the peoples of the earth, and sent your blessed Son to preach peace to those who are far off and to those who are near: Grant that people everywhere may seek after you and find you; bring the nations into your fold; pour out your Spirit upon all flesh; and hasten the coming of your kingdom; through Jesus Christ our Lord. Amen.

(Anglican Church in North America Book of Common Prayer)

Advent Day 10

TAMARA HILL MURPHY

Read: *Luke 16:19–31*

"There was a rich man who was clothed in purple and fine linen and who feasted sumptuously every day. And at his gate was laid a poor man named Lazarus, covered with sores, who desired to be fed with what fell from the rich man's table. Moreover, even the dogs came and licked his sores.

The poor man died and was carried by the angels to Abraham's side. The rich man also died and was buried, and in Hades, being in torment, he lifted up his eyes and saw Abraham far off and Lazarus at his side. And he called out, 'Father Abraham, have mercy on me, and send Lazarus to dip the end of his finger in water and cool my tongue, for I am in anguish in this flame.'

But Abraham said, 'Child, remember that you in your lifetime received your good things, and Lazarus in like manner bad things; but now he is comforted here, and you are in anguish. And besides all this, between us and you a great chasm has been fixed, in order that those who would pass from here to you may not be able, and none may cross from there to us.'

And he said, 'Then I beg you, father, to send him to my father's house—for I have five brothers—so that he may warn them, lest they also come into this place of torment.' But Abraham said, 'They have Moses and the Prophets; let them hear them.' And he said, 'No, father Abraham, but if someone goes to them from the dead, they will repent.' He said to him, 'If they do not hear Moses and the Prophets, neither will they be convinced if someone should rise from the dead.'"

Reflect:

When faced with Christ's words on money and possessions, we may be tempted to do exegetical backflips to make the verses mean something other than money and possessions. Whenever Scripture focuses on wealth, it may refer to *more* than money and possessions, but it never means less.

At the base of biblical justice is the teaching that Jesus gives about money. Time after time, Jesus teaches that wealth belongs to us and yet does not. The Bible insists that all our money belongs to God. Jesus makes sure we don't miss this point by coming at the subject from every angle possible. There may not be a starker warning than the story of the rich man and the beggar Lazarus. Jesus wants all who will listen to recognize exactly what is at stake.

As you pray, allow yourself to read the story of the rich man and Lazarus with an open heart and an open mind. Notice if resistance or defensiveness rises within you. Ask the merciful God, who "stands at the right hand of the needy" (Psalm 109:31 NIV), to reveal what is underneath the defensiveness. Is it fear or shame or blame? Know that when God brings conviction, the Spirit will make clear to your whole self—body, mind, and spirit—how to repent. Listen for that clear direction from our faithful God.

Where there is clarity, confess your sin, receive the cleansing forgiveness of Christ, and trust the Spirit to help you make restitution. If you're able to sit quietly without distraction, notice your breathing, and occasionally breathe in while saying, "Lord Jesus Christ, Son of God," and exhale, saying, "have mercy on me the sinner." Repeat until your heart is settled.

Conclude this time by reading these comforting words from Isaiah, giving thanks for God's faithful love.

Pray:

"I have seen their ways, but I will heal them; I will guide them and restore comfort to Israel's mourners, creating praise on their lips. Peace, peace, to those far and near," says the LORD. "And I will heal them." Amen.

(Isaiah 57:18–19 NIV)

Advent Day 11

TAMARA HILL MURPHY

Read: *Isaiah 58:6–11*

Is not this the fast that I choose:
    to loose the bonds of wickedness,
    to undo the straps of the yoke,
to let the oppressed go free,
    and to break every yoke?
Is it not to share your bread with the hungry
    and bring the homeless poor into your house;
when you see the naked, to cover him,
    and not to hide yourself from your own flesh?
Then shall your light break forth like the dawn,
    and your healing shall spring up speedily;
your righteousness shall go before you;
    the glory of the LORD shall be your rear guard.
Then you shall call, and the LORD will answer;
    you shall cry, and he will say, "Here I am."
If you take away the yoke from your midst,
    the pointing of the finger, and speaking wickedness,
if you pour yourself out for the hungry
    and satisfy the desire of the afflicted,
then shall your light rise in the darkness
    and your gloom be as the noonday.
And the LORD will guide you continually
    and satisfy your desire in scorched places
    and make your bones strong;
and you shall be like a watered garden,
    like a spring of water,
    whose waters do not fail.

Reflect:

Worshipping God in spirit and truth leads us to ask what we can do to show our devotion. The practice of fasting and repentance is one way. But God is clear that fasting and the rituals we associate with religious devotion are only the first steps. They are only the beginning.

The fasting God chooses unleashes a vision beyond our private devotion and even our congregational practices of worship. God desires an allegiance that brings about the wide and deep realities of his vision of justice. Worship moves from private prayer to Sunday sanctuary and then out into the neighborhoods, workplaces, and cities. No piece of rubble is left untended in God's desire for wholeness.

In God's radical generosity, he makes a way for those who've lived in ruin to become repairers, rebuilders, and restorers of a just and beautiful city. In God's miraculous economy, the rubble of our past lives is the material we're given to work into the new foundations of a glorious, renewed community. Not only that, but God's radical generosity also shares the glory with those who help him rebuild. "You'll be known as those who can fix anything" (Isaiah 58:12 MSG). Have you heard anything more preposterous or more wonderful?

All of it—the radical, justice-forming, and glory-sharing generosity of God—propels us from a beginner's religious practice to a full-throated, fully embodied hallelujah!

Begin your time of prayer by considering the words of the psalmist: "From dawn to dusk, keep lifting all your praises to GOD!" (Psalm 113:3 MSG). Ask the Holy Spirit to help you think back over the past year. If that feels overwhelming to you, then focus on one month or just today. When has God picked you up? Rescued you? Treated you as an honored guest? What ruin or rubble from this time might God be inviting you to offer for rebuilding?

Give thanks, and rest in the assurance of our good, restoring God.

Pray:
Father, thank you for lifting me out of the slimy pit, out of the mud and mire. Thank you for setting my feet on a rock and giving me a firm place to stand. Amen.

(adapted from *Psalm 40:2*)

Advent Day 12

TAMARA HILL MURPHY

Read: *Isaiah 59:9–10, 14–17*

> Therefore justice is far from us,
>> and righteousness does not overtake us;
> we hope for light, and behold, darkness,
>> and for brightness, but we walk in gloom.
> We grope for the wall like the blind;
>> we grope like those who have no eyes;
> we stumble at noon as in the twilight,
>> among those in full vigor we are like dead men....
> Justice is turned back,
>> and righteousness stands far away;
> for truth has stumbled in the public squares,
>> and uprightness cannot enter.
> Truth is lacking,
>> and he who departs from evil makes himself a prey.
> The LORD saw it, and it displeased him
>> that there was no justice.
> He saw that there was no man,
>> and wondered that there was no one to intercede;
> then his own arm brought him salvation,
>> and his righteousness upheld him.
> He put on righteousness as a breastplate,
>> and a helmet of salvation on his head;
> he put on garments of vengeance for clothing,
>> and wrapped himself in zeal as a cloak.

Reflect:

Today's passage moves between the visible and invisible realities of a world in desperate need of rescue. In Isaiah, we see what's missing. The prophet lamented that within the places where humankind lives, there's no room for justice, righteousness, or truth. In this cramped, dark abode, humans grope along the walls, blindly searching for a bright and lighted space.

The Lord looks into human structures we have built, but he finds only self-serving spaces; he finds no justice. Offended and incredulous, the Lord intervenes. Is there a better description of a savior than one who puts "on righteousness as body armor, and a helmet of salvation on his head . . . garments of vengeance for clothing, and he wrap[s] himself in zeal as in a cloak" (Isaiah 59:17 csb)?

In Jesus, God broke open the cramped, dark spaces built by human blindness and hubris. The invisible God took on visible flesh, embodying all the immutable attributes of God within skin, blood, and bones. The Redeemer keeps God's covenant and came to restore a beautiful Zion.

Still, many choose to grope along blindly. Still, the space of God's kingdom must be entered to be truly seen.

In prayer, ask God to open the eyes of your heart to discern both the visible and invisible work of the Spirit in you, amid you, and through you. Consider the spaces within and without where Christ is bringing God's kingdom to earth, as it is in heaven. Give thanks for the invitation to stride freely in the spacious place Christ has opened to us.

Pray:

Sovereign Lord, as you have promised, you may now dismiss your servant in peace. For my eyes have seen your salvation, which you have prepared in the sight of all nations: a light for revelation to the Gentiles, and the glory of your people Israel.

(Luke 2:28–32 NIV)

Advent Day 13

NATHAN BAXTER

Read: *Isaiah 60:1–5, 17–19*

> Arise, shine, for your light has come,
>> and the glory of the LORD has risen upon you.
> For behold, darkness shall cover the earth,
>> and thick darkness the peoples;
> but the LORD will arise upon you,
>> and his glory will be seen upon you.
> And nations shall come to your light,
>> and kings to the brightness of your rising.
> Lift up your eyes all around, and see;
>> they all gather together, they come to you;
> your sons shall come from afar,
>> and your daughters shall be carried on the hip.
> Then you shall see and be radiant;
>> your heart shall thrill and exult,
> because the abundance of the sea shall be turned to you,
>> the wealth of the nations shall come to you....
> I will make your overseers peace
>> and your taskmasters righteousness.
> Violence shall no more be heard in your land,
>> devastation or destruction within your borders;
> you shall call your walls Salvation,
>> and your gates Praise.
> The sun shall be no more
>> your light by day,
> nor for brightness shall the moon
>> give you light;
> but the LORD will be your everlasting light,
>> and your God will be your glory.

Reflect:

In this passage, God invites us to leave behind the world east of Eden and to lift up our eyes. "Lift up your eyes all around, and see." God invites—even commands—an extended exercise of holy imagination. This is not an exercise of fantasy or wishful thinking. It is an exercise rooted in God's promises and sure power.

Lift up your eyes and see the restoration of broken families scattered by the exile of sin. Let "your heart . . . throb and swell with joy" (v. 5 NIV).

Let visions of reconciliation among peoples and nations unfold where hostilities have ceased. "They all gather together" (v. 4 NIV). Let hard-to-fathom possibilities unfold before the eyes of your heart.

Look at familiar ruins and think of them resituated in the heavenly city. The work of partial creation, wrecked by the fall and marooned in history, will be brought to full completion.

Gravity is reversed. Weeping becomes joy. With safety beyond threats, peace beyond foreboding, honor beyond any degradation, let visions of God's peace pass before your eyes and beyond your understanding.

Above all, God fills all in all, and finally creation is a worthy vessel for his splendorous light. This is our future, not simply the absence of darkness but the fullness of God's glory. Let us praise him together!

Pray:

O God, you are able to do exceedingly and abundantly beyond all that we ask or imagine, and you purpose to manifest your glory in Christ Jesus and in your church. Expand our imagination so completely that we may find deep hope. Surprise us with your joy when you exceed all our hopes with your glory. In Jesus's name. Amen.

(adapted from Ephesians 3:20–21)

Advent Day 14
TAMARA HILL MURPHY

Read: *Isaiah 61:1–6*

    The Spirit of the Lord God is upon me,
        because the Lord has anointed me
    to bring good news to the poor;
        he has sent me to bind up the brokenhearted,
    to proclaim liberty to the captives,
        and the opening of the prison to those who are bound;
    to proclaim the year of the Lord's favor,
        and the day of vengeance of our God;
        to comfort all who mourn;
    to grant to those who mourn in Zion—
        to give them a beautiful headdress instead of ashes,
    the oil of gladness instead of mourning,
        the garment of praise instead of a faint spirit;
    that they may be called oaks of righteousness,
        the planting of the Lord, that he may be glorified.
    They shall build up the ancient ruins;
        they shall raise up the former devastations;
    they shall repair the ruined cities,
        the devastations of many generations.
    Strangers shall stand and tend your flocks;
        foreigners shall be your plowmen and vinedressers;
    but you shall be called the priests of the Lord;
        they shall speak of you as the ministers of our God;
    you shall eat the wealth of the nations,
        and in their glory you shall boast.

Reflect:

Could there be a more astounding climax to the Old and New Testament readings from the past several days than Isaiah 61? God gave Isaiah the script for the first message Jesus would ever preach; in the synagogue the scroll was unfurled in the human hands of the Son of God: "The Spirit of the Lord

40

GOD is upon me . . . I will greatly rejoice in the LORD; my soul shall exult in my God" (vv. 1, 10).

Sometimes the lectionary pairs Isaiah's powerful prophecy with Mary's prophetic anthem in Luke: "My soul magnifies the Lord, and my spirit rejoices in God my Savior" (Luke 1:46–47).

The same Spirit anoints us all to bring good news to the poor, bind up the brokenhearted, proclaim liberty to the captives, open up the prisons, comfort all who mourn, build up the ancient ruins, and repair the ruined cities, the devastations of many generations. Isaiah proclaimed to us our special call: "But you shall be called the priests of the LORD" (Isaiah 61:6).

As part or all of your prayer, take time to be silent, without any noise or distraction, and to pause and meditate on these words. There's no need to strive for a profound insight during this time. Just be still.

If you begin to sense thoughts or feelings bubbling up in the quiet, notice them without trying to analyze. You might breathe out one phrase each time you're tempted to become distracted: "My soul magnifies the Lord" (Luke 1:46) or "The Spirit of the Lord GOD is upon me" (Isaiah 61:1).

Trust God as your heavenly Father to be present with you through Christ and by his Spirit. End your time with a simple prayer or chorus. Go in peace.

Pray:
(Silence)

Advent Day 15
ABIGAIL HULL WHITEHOUSE

Read: *Isaiah 62:1–5, 12*

> For Zion's sake I will not keep silent,
>   and for Jerusalem's sake I will not be quiet,
> until her righteousness goes forth as brightness,
>   and her salvation as a burning torch.
> The nations shall see your righteousness,
>   and all the kings your glory,
> and you shall be called by a new name
>   that the mouth of the LORD will give.
> You shall be a crown of beauty in the hand of the LORD,
>   and a royal diadem in the hand of your God.
> You shall no more be termed Forsaken,
>   and your land shall no more be termed Desolate,
> but you shall be called My Delight Is in Her,
>   and your land Married;
> for the LORD delights in you,
>   and your land shall be married.
> For as a young man marries a young woman,
>   so shall your sons marry you,
> and as the bridegroom rejoices over the bride,
>   so shall your God rejoice over you....
> And they shall be called The Holy People,
>   The Redeemed of the LORD;
> and you shall be called Sought Out,
>   A City Not Forsaken.

Reflect:

Names have the power to define us and to shape our destinies. We know this from personal experience and also from God's Word. Throughout Scripture, God would change people's names in order to indicate a new season or calling. Often, it was an invitation to step into a deeper, truer identity that the individual could not yet fully comprehend: Abram became Abraham, the father of many; Saul became Paul, the humble servant of the gospel; and Simon Peter became Cephas, the rock on which the church is built.

We see something similar in this passage. Rather than be termed "Forsaken" or "Desolate," Zion shall be called "Married," the object of God's delight (v. 4), a people "Sought Out" and "A City Not Forsaken" (v. 12). The prophet wanted the people of God to know that their current circumstances did not define them and were not the final word. Rather, God has a destiny for his people, and he was calling them to step into it by embracing their identity as his beloved.

What names are you wearing today? As God's covenant ones, purchased by the blood of the Lamb, we can and should appropriate the names we find in Isaiah 62:12: We are the Holy People, the Redeemed of the Lord, the ones who are Sought Out and Not Forsaken.

Regardless of our circumstances or the raggedness we might feel, God says that we are a "crown of beauty" and like royal diadems sparkling in his hands (v. 3). Do you believe this to be true? Or is there something in the way—some stone you need to clear—in order for you to hear the Lord speak these loving words over you?

Take a moment now to invite the Lord to be present with you and to bring anything to mind that you need to confess. Turn it all over to him.

Reread the passage for this day and ask the Holy Spirit to highlight if there is a name he wants to give you for this season ahead.

Pray:

Father, thank you that the truest thing about us is not what we see or experience but what you say about us in your Word. Give us the grace to believe that we are your beloved and that we have been made radiant by Christ's dying and rising. Help us to shed our false selves and to live as your sought-out and redeemed people. In your Son's precious and powerful name, and by your Spirit. Amen.

Advent Day 16

MADISON PERRY

Read: *Isaiah 63:7–9*

> I will recount the steadfast love of the LORD,
>> the praises of the LORD,
> according to all that the LORD has granted us,
>> and the great goodness to the house of Israel
> that he has granted them according to his compassion,
>> according to the abundance of his steadfast love.
> For he said, "Surely they are my people,
>> children who will not deal falsely."
> And he became their Savior.
> In all their affliction he was afflicted,
>> and the angel of his presence saved them;
> in his love and in his pity he redeemed them;
>> he lifted them up and carried them all the days of old.

Reflect:

"And he became their Savior. In all their affliction he was afflicted."

This passage in Isaiah tells of the warrior God who has trampled evil and wrought this victory. He has become our Savior!

And what kind of salvation do we seek?

We seek salvation from oppression. From injustice. And ultimately from the darkness that we have held close to ourselves.

As we consider God's cosmic victory and rejoice in the outworking of his justice, it is all too easy to think of the evil external to us, but even in this passage we see how we have been complicit in our own tragedy. We did not defeat evil, but nonetheless victory has been amazingly accomplished.

During this season, we remember what the start of God's salvation looks like: the miraculous birth of a child. Without God, we have no cause for hope within the outworking of natural history. Hope is not derived from the power of our best intentions. But God has become our Savior!

We have seen the outworking of God's rescue through the birth, death, and resurrection of Jesus, and we can surely say, "I will recount the steadfast love of the LORD." Great goodness has come to us. As you go to prayer with this passage, begin by praising the One who, alone, won victory.

Pray:

Lord Jesus, Lamb of God, you alone won victory over evil—even mine—and you are worthy because you were slain and, with your blood, you purchased for God persons from every tribe and language and people and nation, even those who abandoned you to fight alone in your kindness for the salvation of the world. I bow to your wisdom and grace. Amen.

Advent Day 17

ABIGAIL HULL WHITEHOUSE

Read: *Isaiah 64:1–8*

> Oh that you would rend the heavens and come down,
>> that the mountains might quake at your presence—
> as when fire kindles brushwood
>> and the fire causes water to boil—
> to make your name known to your adversaries,
>> and that the nations might tremble at your presence!
> When you did awesome things that we did not look for,
>> you came down, the mountains quaked at your presence.
> From of old no one has heard
>> or perceived by the ear,
> no eye has seen a God besides you,
>> who acts for those who wait for him.
> You meet him who joyfully works righteousness,
>> those who remember you in your ways.
> Behold, you were angry, and we sinned;
>> in our sins we have been a long time, and shall we be saved?
> We have all become like one who is unclean,
>> and all our righteous deeds are like a polluted garment.
> We all fade like a leaf, and our iniquities, like the wind, take
>> us away.
> There is no one who calls upon your name,
>> who rouses himself to take hold of you;
> for you have hidden your face from us,
>> and have made us melt in the hand of our iniquities.
> But now, O Lord, you are our Father;
>> we are the clay, and you are our potter;
>> we are all the work of your hand.

Reflect:

In our reading from Isaiah 64, the prophet pleaded for God to "come down"—to intervene in the life of his people like fire kindling brush or boiling water.

He reminded the people of how God did "awesome things that [they] did not look for" (v. 3) in the past, and then he went on to say these words: "No eye has seen a God besides you, who acts for those who wait for him" (v. 4).

The prophet reminded us that God acts on behalf of his people. He does not sit idly by; he does not slumber or sleep. Rather, he *intervenes* in the life of his people in very active ways to protect and provide. Like the guard at a castle gate, God keeps us, watching our very going out and coming in. Nothing escapes his notice; there is a deep security in the knowledge of his providential protection and care.

But the prophet also reminded us that God acts for those *who wait for him*. Waiting involves ceding control, surrendering timelines, actively resisting the impulse to move on our own, and instead looking to the God who moves on our behalf. Waiting involves hope, trust, and persistent prayer.

As you sit with difficult situations in your own life and in our world—with all that is unfinished, uncertain, and waiting to be resolved—invite God to become present to you and to all that you are carrying. Where do you need God to act this Advent? Where does the waiting feel especially hard? Ask God for the courage and grace to wait and to trust that he will provide in due season. Remember the times in your life when God did awesome things that you did not look for, and expect him to be faithful again. Submit your requests in faith, knowing that your keeper is watching over you, your loved ones, and our world in the waiting.

Pray:

Heavenly Father, you have promised to hear what we ask in the Name of your Son: Accept and fulfill our petitions, we pray, not as we ask in our ignorance, nor as we deserve in our sinfulness, but as you know and love us in your Son Jesus Christ our Lord. Amen.

(Anglican Church in North America Book of Common Prayer)

Advent Day 18
SALLY BREEDLOVE

Read: *Lamentations 3:19–30*

Remember my affliction and my wanderings,
   the wormwood and the gall!
My soul continually remembers it
   and is bowed down within me.
But this I call to mind,
   and therefore I have hope:
The steadfast love of the LORD never ceases;
   his mercies never come to an end;
they are new every morning;
   great is your faithfulness.
"The LORD is my portion," says my soul,
   "therefore I will hope in him."
The LORD is good to those who wait for him,
   to the soul who seeks him.
It is good that one should wait quietly
   for the salvation of the LORD.
It is good for a man that he bear
   the yoke in his youth.
Let him sit alone in silence
   when it is laid on him;
let him put his mouth in the dust—
   there may yet be hope;
let him give his cheek to the one who strikes,
   and let him be filled with insults.

Reflect:

"The 'worst' is never the worst" (Lamentations 3:30 MSG). "Wait for hope to appear" (v. 29 MSG). "GOD's loyal love couldn't have run out" (v. 22 MSG).

The prophet Jeremiah was likely the one who offered these promises to the Jewish people as their world fell apart. Jerusalem was razed and the nation obliterated. Every educated and wealthy person had been hauled off to captivity in Babylon. All appeared to be lost. Five poems of heartbreaking lament fill this book of the Bible.

But Lamentations is not a book of despair. Rather, it's an honest speaking of agony, confusion, and anger. It was true that the pain Jerusalem was suffering was the result of a shattering loss. Things would never be the same, but Lamentations proclaims that the Lord is mightier and more beautiful than every loss.

Are you in a season with much to lament? The Bible takes the lead in teaching you how to speak honestly. Name your sorrows and your losses.

In your lament, remember that you are talking to the one who is more real than your grief or your fears. The mighty eternal God, who is Father, Son, and Holy Spirit, will never walk out on you and refuse to return. He is here as Immanuel in the midst of it all. He will one day make "all things new" as Revelation 21:5 promises.

When you sense you have spoken your heart, be still for a moment. God accepts you as you are. As best you can, pray that your hope grows and that your courage grows. Who do you know who is lost in sadness or fear? Pray for that person to know the loyal love of God in new ways. Pray you become the kind of person who offers a calm, fixed hope to others.

Pray:

Lord Jesus Christ, you stretched out your arms of love on the hard wood of the cross that everyone might come within the reach of your saving embrace: So clothe us in your Spirit that we, reaching forth our hands in love, may bring those who do not know you to the knowledge and love of you; for the honor of your Name. Amen.

(Anglican Church in North America Book of Common Prayer)

Advent Day 19

MADISON PERRY

Read: *Isaiah 65:17–23*

"For behold, I create new heavens
 and a new earth,
and the former things shall not be remembered
 or come into mind.
But be glad and rejoice forever
 in that which I create;
for behold, I create Jerusalem to be a joy,
 and her people to be a gladness.
I will rejoice in Jerusalem
 and be glad in my people;
no more shall be heard in it the sound of weeping
 and the cry of distress.
No more shall there be in it
 an infant who lives but a few days,
 or an old man who does not fill out his days,
for the young man shall die a hundred years old,
 and the sinner a hundred years old shall be accursed.
They shall build houses and inhabit them;
 they shall plant vineyards and eat their fruit.
They shall not build and another inhabit;
 they shall not plant and another eat;
for like the days of a tree shall the days of my people be,
 and my chosen shall long enjoy the work of their hands.
They shall not labor in vain
 or bear children for calamity,
for they shall be the offspring of the blessed of the Lord,
 and their descendants with them."

Reflect:

The promise of God's salvation is a promise of new heavens and new earth. No longer shall the former things come to mind. No longer shall there be tragedy or tears.

Is this good news to you? Are you tired of the former things? Are you ready to shrug off the evils of the present age? Are you ready to leave behind the constraints of a life bound by your mistakes and the thousands of disappointments that every person knows?

Or maybe the thought of a new world is unsettling because in many ways you already feel at home. It could be that your world seems stable. But even if this is your story, you suspect you inhabit a fragile peace, one that could be shattered by the movement of the minute hand or with the ringing of your phone.

Leave behind what haunts you and consider the new heavens and the new earth. Together we shall inhabit houses, plant vineyards, and live to see the blessed prosperity of our children. Together we shall be God's delight, and we shall praise our great God.

Pray:

O God our King, by the resurrection of your Son Jesus Christ on the first day of the week, you conquered sin, put death to flight, and gave us the hope of everlasting life: Redeem all our days by this victory; forgive our sins, banish our fears, make us bold to praise you and to do your will; and steel us to wait for the consummation of your kingdom on the last great Day; through Jesus Christ our Lord. Amen.

(Anglican Church in North America Book of Common Prayer)

Advent Day 20
SALLY BREEDLOVE

Read: *Malachi 3:13–18*

"Your words have been hard against me, says the LORD. But you say, 'How have we spoken against you?' You have said, 'It is vain to serve God. What is the profit of our keeping his charge or of walking as in mourning before the LORD of hosts? And now we call the arrogant blessed. Evildoers not only prosper but they put God to the test and they escape.'"

Then those who feared the LORD spoke with one another. The LORD paid attention and heard them, and a book of remembrance was written before him of those who feared the LORD and esteemed his name. "They shall be mine, says the LORD of hosts, in the day when I make up my treasured possession, and I will spare them as a man spares his son who serves him. Then once more you shall see the distinction between the righteous and the wicked, between one who serves God and one who does not serve him."

Reflect:

Malachi 3 overflows with tension. God's people have become his detractors. What happened? They were angry because it seemed as though keeping God's rules hadn't done them any good. Their lives were just as hard as the lives of those who ignored God. Furthermore, the very definitions of faith, morality, and ethics were under attack, undermined by the scorn of the unbelieving world. God's people were on the defensive.

We, too, live in a world where God is being charged with crime after crime and where Christians are seen as the problem. Who hasn't struggled with holding on to the teachings that used to be accepted by the majority but are now scorned by many? Who hasn't questioned God's ways in this world?

Doubt and struggle are normal for people who live by faith, but how do we resist putting God on the witness stand? What do we do instead? Let Malachi 3:16 teach us: "Then those who feared the LORD spoke with one another."

Our world is upside down with violence, side-taking, blaming, and contempt. More than ever, those who love God need to talk with each other.

As you pray, ask yourself, "Who could I call?" Who needs the encouragement of your friendship and your faith (no matter how weak it seems to you)? Is there something God has taught you that you sense you are to share with another person? Pray for that person and that conversation. Make that call. We need each other.

In this season of Advent, hold your own heart close to God's promises. The people who encourage each other in the faith, Malachi says, are God's treasure. They are children of the heavenly Father. They will be spared on the day of God's wrath.

Let your heart be at peace.

Pray:

Gracious God and most merciful Father, you have granted us the rich and precious jewel of your holy Word: Assist us with your Spirit, that the same Word may be written in our hearts to our everlasting comfort, to reform us, to renew us according to your own image, to build us up and edify us into the perfect dwelling place of your Christ, sanctifying and increasing in us all heavenly virtues; grant this, O heavenly Father, for Jesus Christ's sake. Amen.

(Anglican Church in North America Book of Common Prayer)

Advent Day 21
SALLY BREEDLOVE

Read: *Malachi 4*

"For behold, the day is coming, burning like an oven, when all the arrogant and all evildoers will be stubble. The day that is coming shall set them ablaze," says the LORD of hosts, so that it will leave them neither root nor branch. But for you who fear my name, the sun of righteousness shall rise with healing in its wings. You shall go out leaping like calves from the stall. And you shall tread down the wicked, for they will be ashes under the soles of your feet, on the day when I act," says the LORD of hosts.

"Remember the law of my servant Moses, the statutes and rules that I commanded him at Horeb for all Israel.

"Behold, I will send you Elijah the prophet before the great and awesome day of the LORD comes. And he will turn the hearts of fathers to their children and the hearts of children to their fathers, lest I come and strike the land with a decree of utter destruction."

Reflect:

Pause a moment and allow yourself to imagine these realities:

- Pride and evil done away with, until no darkness remains.
- All wrong vanished to less than ashes like the powdery dust that is left from a fiercely hot oven.
- Health and energy restored so you feel young again, ready to tackle anything.
- A true north orientation for your whole life because the ancient words God gave Moses make sense to you.
- Families restored, so fathers love their children and sacrifice for them, and children are filled to the brim by the attention of their fathers.

Could all these good things possibly come true?

Malachi wasn't daydreaming. He was declaring God's promises to us. A day is coming when one good thing will overtake the next. This coming day will be more than a new era. It will be life itself.

Wonderfully, Malachi didn't say, "Work to make these things happen." That ought to relieve us. The complexity and brokenness of our world is everywhere. We know we can't manufacture a societal change of this magnitude or legislate it into being.

So, what's our response to the problems we live with as we seek to hold on to the promises of God? Do we do nothing until God sets things right?

Not at all. Today matters. As the apostle Peter put it, "Since everything here today might well be gone tomorrow, do you see how essential it is to live a holy life? Daily expect the Day of God, eager for its arrival" (2 Peter 3:11–12 MSG).

As you pray, thank your heavenly Father that one day all will be utterly made right. In this season of active waiting, ask him to show you how to live a holy life that anticipates his coming. Ask him to show you just one thing that you can repent of and change.

Pray:
O Lord, help me to live this day for that day. For Jesus's sake. Amen.

Advent Day 22

ELIZABETH GATEWOOD

Read: *Isaiah 24:16–21, 23*

From the ends of the earth we hear songs of praise,
of glory to the Righteous One.
But I say, "I waste away,
I waste away. Woe is me!
For the traitors have betrayed,
with betrayal the traitors have betrayed."
Terror and the pit and the snare
are upon you, O inhabitant of the earth!
He who flees at the sound of the terror
shall fall into the pit,
and he who climbs out of the pit
shall be caught in the snare.
For the windows of heaven are opened,
and the foundations of the earth tremble.
The earth is utterly broken,
the earth is split apart,
the earth is violently shaken.
The earth staggers like a drunken man;
it sways like a hut;
its transgression lies heavy upon it,
and it falls, and will not rise again.
On that day the Lord will punish
the host of heaven, in heaven,
and the kings of the earth, on the earth….
Then the moon will be confounded
and the sun ashamed,
for the Lord of hosts reigns
on Mount Zion and in Jerusalem,
and his glory will be before his elders.

Reflect:

Isaiah's prophecy of judgment and destruction seems to flip between different explanations for and responses to this coming judgment.

Is it God who causes calamity? Or is it the sin of the people—their lawlessness and breaking of the covenant—that has defiled the earth? And what is the proper response? To sing for joy, giving glory to God, or to lament, as Isaiah did in verse 16 of today's passage?

In the middle of these questions is a stark description of the earth's desecration and bitterness. The cities—beacons of civilization and places of refuge and protection—are ruined. The music and dancing—manifestations of the beauty of human culture and imagination—have ceased. The fertility of the earth—necessary for the survival of all life—has been stripped and exhausted. The land is withered.

Who is responsible? Is God? Is Israel? Should they mourn and lament? Should they praise God anyway? The chapter ends not with answers but with a stark affirmation of God's presence and power. God reigns in great glory and power.

As you pray, hold these tensions and ambiguities—in this passage and in your own life—before the Lord.

Pray:

God, ours is a world where joy often turns to gloom with the grief of lives lost, disease, natural disasters, and fractured relationships. Are we responsible? Are you, God? Should we lament, or should we keep praising you anyway? Fill our mouths and hearts with both words of lament and words of praise. Give us courage to do the work that is ours to do for the healing of the world. Amen.

Advent Day 23
ELIZABETH GATEWOOD

Read: *Isaiah 25:1, 3–9*

O Lord, you are my God;
    I will exalt you; I will praise your name,
for you have done wonderful things,
plans formed of old, faithful and sure....
Therefore strong peoples will glorify you;
    cities of ruthless nations will fear you.
For you have been a stronghold to the poor,
    a stronghold to the needy in his distress,
    a shelter from the storm and a shade from the heat;
for the breath of the ruthless is like a storm against a wall,
    like heat in a dry place.
You subdue the noise of the foreigners;
    as heat by the shade of a cloud,
    so the song of the ruthless is put down.
On this mountain the Lord of hosts will make for all peoples
    a feast of rich food, a feast of well-aged wine,
    of rich food full of marrow, of aged wine well refined.
And he will swallow up on this mountain
    the covering that is cast over all peoples,
    the veil that is spread over all nations.
    He will swallow up death forever;
and the Lord God will wipe away tears from all faces,
    and the reproach of his people he will take away from all
the earth,
    for the Lord has spoken.
It will be said on that day,
    "Behold, this is our God; we have waited for him, that he
might save us.
    This is the Lord; we have waited for him;
    let us be glad and rejoice in his salvation."

Reflect:

Isaiah described the redemption of the world as a rich banquet, one with the best wine and the best meat. But this is no stiff corporate dinner with fine food but dull conversation. The best part of this feast are the guests. All people will gather at this banquet table. And there will be no tears. The world will be healed and made new.

We live in the tension between these vibrant promises and our difficult daily existence. Perhaps the redemption that Isaiah described feels like a far-off dream to you. As we move deeper into this Advent season, we sense more and more the tension between hope in the Lord and longing for the fulfillment of his promises, between the felt pain of our world and the desire for its future restoration.

Take a moment and let these words settle in your heart and mind.

Ask the Lord how to live well within these realities. As you pray, name your griefs and longings before the Lord. Pray for redemption in specific areas. Thank God for his promise to restore all things.

Pray:

God, is it true that you are capable of wiping away all tears? The tears of a wife abandoned and disgraced by her husband? The tears of families pressing their hands together against hospital windows? The tears of children in detention facilities who may never see their parents again? The tears of broken relationships, economic hardship, disease? If you can do it, why not now? Lord, we long for your heavenly banquet. We long to feast with all peoples at the table of your abundance. Come quickly, Lord Jesus. Set the banquet table. Wipe our tears. We are ready. Amen.

Advent Day 24

ELIZABETH GATEWOOD

Read: *Luke 1:26–38*

In the sixth month the angel Gabriel was sent from God to a city of Galilee named Nazareth, to a virgin betrothed to a man whose name was Joseph, of the house of David. And the virgin's name was Mary. And he came to her and said, "Greetings, O favored one, the Lord is with you!" But she was greatly troubled at the saying, and tried to discern what sort of greeting this might be. And the angel said to her, "Do not be afraid, Mary, for you have found favor with God. And behold, you will conceive in your womb and bear a son, and you shall call his name Jesus. He will be great and will be called the Son of the Most High. And the Lord God will give to him the throne of his father David, and he will reign over the house of Jacob forever, and of his kingdom there will be no end."

And Mary said to the angel, "How will this be, since I am a virgin?"

And the angel answered her, "The Holy Spirit will come upon you, and the power of the Most High will overshadow you; therefore the child to be born will be called holy—the Son of God. And behold, your relative Elizabeth in her old age has also conceived a son, and this is the sixth month with her who was called barren. For nothing will be impossible with God." And Mary said, "Behold, I am the servant of the Lord; let it be to me according to your word." And the angel departed from her.

Reflect:

Ask any woman who has been pregnant, and she will tell you what a strange experience it is to have your body invaded and overcome by new life. It starts invisibly, with fatigue and nausea. It's a strange thing to suddenly have your capacities for productivity drastically diminished. As new life grows, clothes become uncomfortable and unwearable. Prior activities and indulgences seem impossible. It is a small grief not to be able to take a long bike ride or enjoy a sushi dinner with friends.

A mother, her body uniquely strong and generative, becomes weak even in the beautiful exhibition of her strength.

We long for the gospel to enter our lives in scheduled and controlled ways. We try to tame and rationalize its wilder demands and invitations. And yet Jesus breaks into our lives and our world with explosive new life.

Mary welcomed it—the weakness of motherhood and the explosiveness of the gospel—with humility and joy.

As you pray, consider in what ways you are tempted to package the gospel as a consumer item that fits in with your lifestyle. Pray for God to reveal to you where you may be missing his presence and his invitations to new life.

Pray:

God, we would prefer to have some control over how you transform our lives and hearts. We have goals and plans. We have busy schedules. We have careers and obligations. We want to tame and contain your presence and your invitations because they are too much for us. In this season of Advent, let us be more like Mary, who welcomed the chaos and inconvenience of Jesus with joy and openness. Let us learn from the women around us who courageously become weak to bring new life into the world. Show us where we need to surrender pieces of ourselves to give room for you and your transformative presence in the world. Give us the strength of Mary to be weak, to be overcome by your new life. Amen.

Advent Day 25
ELIZABETH GATEWOOD

Read: *Luke 1:57–64, 67, 76–79*

Now the time came for Elizabeth to give birth, and she bore a son. And her neighbors and relatives heard that the Lord had shown great mercy to her, and they rejoiced with her. And on the eighth day they came to circumcise the child. And they would have called him Zechariah after his father, but his mother answered, "No; he shall be called John." And they said to her, "None of your relatives is called by this name." And they made signs to his father, inquiring what he wanted him to be called. And he asked for a writing tablet and wrote, "His name is John." And they all wondered. And immediately his mouth was opened and his tongue loosed, and he spoke, blessing God….

And his father Zechariah was filled with the Holy Spirit and prophesied, saying,…

"And you, child, will be called the prophet of the Most High;
for you will go before the Lord to prepare his ways,
to give knowledge of salvation to his people
in the forgiveness of their sins,
because of the tender mercy of our God,
whereby the sunrise shall visit us from on high
to give light to those who sit in darkness and in the shadow of
death, to guide our feet into the way of peace."

Reflect:

After a strange and humbling season of muteness, Zechariah's voice returned. He met his infant son, John, and introduced him to the world. And we read that this strange news—a mute father made to speak again, an angel-promised baby—captured the minds of the people who heard about it. After etching John's name and receiving his voice back, Zechariah perhaps said a few repentant or wry words to his wife, who had just given birth. Then he offered a beautiful prophecy and benediction on the life of his son.

John prepared the way for Jesus, plowing the soil of people's hearts and imaginations so that when they met Jesus, they could see him and accept him; the gospel could take root.

During Advent, we are more aware than ever that we live in the "already but not yet," the time after Jesus's life, death, and resurrection but before his second coming to make all things new. And our work is not so different from John's. We, too, are called to go on before the Lord to prepare the way for him. We all have a different vocation and location, but we are each called to make the world new again. We pursue and embody beauty, justice, and truth. We preach the gospel and let our lives be transformed by it. We work for the renewal of people, places, and institutions. We prepare the way for Jesus.

As you pray, hear Zechariah's words as a benediction over your own life and work.

Pray:

God, you place us and call us to specific work for your kingdom. Yet so often our work is a source of frustration, shame, longing, and pain. Would you let us see our work as part of your grand redemption of the world? Teach us from the life of John the Baptist about what it looks like for our lives to point to you. Reveal to us specific ways that our work can embody and proclaim your coming kingdom. Give us creativity, patience, and endurance to do the specific work that you have called us to do. Amen.

Advent Day 26
WILLA KANE

Read: *Isaiah 7:14 & Micah 5:2–5*

> Therefore the Lord himself will give you a sign. Behold, the virgin shall conceive and bear a son, and shall call his name Immanuel.

***

> But you, O Bethlehem Ephrathah,
>   who are too little to be among the clans of Judah,
> from you shall come forth for me
>   one who is to be ruler in Israel,
> whose coming forth is from of old,
>   from ancient days.
> Therefore he shall give them up until the time
>   when she who is in labor has given birth;
> then the rest of his brothers shall return
>   to the people of Israel.
> And he shall stand and shepherd his flock in the strength of the LORD,
>   in the majesty of the name of the LORD his God.
> And they shall dwell secure, for now he shall be great
>   to the ends of the earth.
> And he shall be their peace.

Reflect:

Behold. This common interjection in the Old Testament means "pay attention!" Prophets Isaiah and Micah both called people in Judah to attention during the eighth century BC. They call us to attention as well.

Isaiah's audience in this passage was Judah's King Ahaz, who worshipped idols, practiced child sacrifice, and desecrated the temple. Despite facing united enemy forces from Israel and Syria, Ahaz refused to believe God alone could deliver Judah from its foes.

Isaiah gave a prophetic response to this unbelief: "Therefore the Lord himself will give you a sign. Behold, the virgin shall conceive and bear a son, and shall call his name Immanuel."

Why this message to Ahaz, a prophecy about a miraculous birth that wouldn't happen for seven hundred years? The answer is in a name. Immanuel means "God with us." The child, God incarnate, was a sign that God would be with his people as protector. Behold. God protects his people by doing something much greater than defeating political foes.

While Isaiah spoke to a king, Micah spoke to the poor and downtrodden of the day. His prophecy? Little Bethlehem, not a kingly city, was where the real king, the ruler of Israel, would be born. This king would shepherd and stand in the strength and majesty of the Lord his God. And these people, the poor and downtrodden, would dwell secure because Jesus, the real King, is their peace.

These truths spoken to king and peasants centuries ago, fulfilled in little Bethlehem, are truths for us this Advent.

As you come to pray, kneel toward Bethlehem. Behold the child who would be your Savior, your Shepherd, your King, your Peace.

Pray:

Lord, we await your coming! May we behold you as Savior, Shepherd, and King, now and into eternity. Amen.

Advent Day 27

SALLY BREEDLOVE

Read: *Matthew 1:18–25*

Now the birth of Jesus Christ took place in this way. When his mother Mary had been betrothed to Joseph, before they came together she was found to be with child from the Holy Spirit. And her husband Joseph, being a just man and unwilling to put her to shame, resolved to divorce her quietly. But as he considered these things, behold, an angel of the Lord appeared to him in a dream, saying, "Joseph, son of David, do not fear to take Mary as your wife, for that which is conceived in her is from the Holy Spirit. She will bear a son, and you shall call his name Jesus, for he will save his people from their sins." All this took place to fulfill what the Lord had spoken by the prophet:

"Behold, the virgin shall conceive and bear a son, and they shall call his name Immanuel" (which means, God with us).

When Joseph woke from sleep, he did as the angel of the Lord commanded him: he took his wife, but knew her not until she had given birth to a son. And he called his name Jesus.

Reflect:

Immanuel. This name for Jesus appears only four times in Scripture: In Matthew an angel came to Joseph in a dream, reassuring him that he was to marry his betrothed wife even though she had been found to be with child. From this angel Joseph discovered that the Holy Spirit was the author of this child that grew in the Virgin Mary. Joseph was commanded: name the child Jesus.

Luke lets us in on the fact that Mary was also given the child's name by Gabriel, the angel she encountered. Pause for a moment—Mary and Joseph were on the verge of full marriage in the Jewish culture, but they had this huge and shameful reality staring them down. Mary was pregnant. Yet she clung to her story: She had known no man. Did Joseph doubt his dream and the angel's words? Did he doubt Mary? Did Mary wonder or fear after her encounter with Gabriel? Perhaps, but consider the kindness of God. They learned they had both been instructed to name this child Jesus. We can only imagine the goodness and strength this gave them as they realized that God was indeed alongside them, writing their story.

Matthew's encouragement continues. This child's deeper identity is Immanuel. God with us. In Isaiah 7 and 8 we are told three times that our stubbornness, our wasteful lives, and even the overwhelming evil that comes at us like tidal waves do not have to undo us. God-with-us is the truest thing.

As you live in these unfolding days of Advent, no matter the circumstances of your life, one thing is utterly true: Immanuel. God is with you.

Pray:

Take a moment and hold before your own heart one of the hardest things you are facing. Then finish this sentence: God is with me in _____ .

Christmas Eve
ABIGAIL HULL WHITEHOUSE

Read: *Psalm 134*

> Come, bless the LORD, all you servants of the LORD,
>   who stand by night in the house of the LORD!
> Lift up your hands to the holy place
>   and bless the LORD!
> May the LORD bless you from Zion,
>   he who made heaven and earth!

Reflect:

Our psalm begins with a call to worship. It's as if the psalmist was scurrying around the temple, beckoning all who might hear him to drop what they were doing and engage in worship. In context, the psalmist was summoning the Levitical priests—those servants of the Lord who stood watch in the temple—but this is a perfect summons for us, too, on this Christmas Eve.

Come. Stop what you're doing—all your prepping, planning, and last-minute gift wrapping—and draw near to the God who came close in Christ; dwell with him in these sacred and set-apart moments ahead. Fix your mind, attention, and imagination on him.

And *bless the Lord.* Speak well and wonderfully of our incarnate King.

Let your words be bountiful, gracious, and true as you contemplate his character in prayer. Let your praise pour forth uninhibited.

And *lift up your hands.* Don't limit your worship only to your words!

Lift up your hands! Lift up your voice! Lift up your heart! Let your whole body respond to the God who came as an infant and as an offering. Posture yourself in such a way that worship flows freely through you.

"Come, bless the LORD, all you servants of the LORD, who stand by night in the house of the LORD! Lift up your hands to the holy place and bless the LORD!" (vv. 1–2).

As you pray, offer up the very best and brightest sacrifice of praise to our King, who came and is coming again. Delight yourself in the Lord, and dwell richly with him in this last day of Advent.

Pray:

Our Jesus, root of David, bright morning star, thank you that you dwell with us and dwell in us. Manifest your presence now, our Immanuel. In your most holy name. Amen.

Introduction to Christmastide
STEVEN E. BREEDLOVE

*D*O WE RECOGNIZE WHAT IT MEANS that the eternal Word of God became man?

This, after all, is what the season of Christmas (all twelve days) is about. God became man. This single thought drives a season of pure celebration. We feast during this season not because he died and rose (that comes later) but simply because he became a human being. In the incarnation, God said yes to his creation rather than ridding himself of it. What is more, he said yes to our human nature itself! In Jesus Christ, human nature—even its physicality—was drawn into the life of the Trinity.

This should drive our prayers as we feast during the season of Christmas. God has said yes to creation and to us, and our humanity is now a part of God's own life. As we pray during this season, our prayers should be full of joy, not only because we have not been rejected but also because a way has been made for us to be in the presence of God as we are—creatures in bodies. Like Mary, we should treasure this in our hearts and let it overflow in peace and joy in our prayers as we feast.

Christmastide Day 1
ABIGAIL HULL WHITEHOUSE

Read: *Luke 2:1–14*

In those days a decree went out from Caesar Augustus that all the world should be registered. This was the first registration when Quirinius was governor of Syria. And all went to be registered, each to his own town. And Joseph also went up from Galilee, from the town of Nazareth, to Judea, to the city of David, which is called Bethlehem, because he was of the house and lineage of David, to be registered with Mary, his betrothed, who was with child. And while they were there, the time came for her to give birth. And she gave birth to her firstborn son and wrapped him in swaddling cloths and laid him in a manger, because there was no place for them in the inn.

And in the same region there were shepherds out in the field, keeping watch over their flock by night. And an angel of the Lord appeared to them, and the glory of the Lord shone around them, and they were filled with great fear. And the angel said to them, "Fear not, for behold, I bring you good news of great joy that will be for all the people. For unto you is born this day in the city of David a Savior, who is Christ the Lord. And this will be a sign for you: you will find a baby wrapped in swaddling cloths and lying in a manger." And suddenly there was with the angel a multitude of the heavenly host praising God and saying,

"Glory to God in the highest,
and on earth peace among those with whom he is pleased!"

Reflect:

What would it have been like to be there on the night the angels appeared to the shepherds?

As you read through these familiar words from Luke 2, place yourself in the scene. Imagine what it would have smelled like, looked like, and sounded like to be keeping watch over the flock. Was it cold? Warm? Bright? Still? What does it look like in your mind? Allow yourself to wonder.

Then ask God to help you inhabit this scene and to find your place within it. Where are you on this night? Are you one of the shepherds, or are you an onlooker in the dark? Are you with Mary and Joseph in the stable, or are you somewhere else? Give yourself permission to engage with Scripture in this imaginative way and take some time to locate yourself within this scene. Be open to any of the many ways God might lead or speak.

What strikes you as you sit with this passage? Can you envision the angels or the sound or the feel of the glory shining around them? How do you react to their presence and the news they share? What, if anything, comes to mind as you contemplate this heavenly host?

Linger in this scene and take note of any words, images, or impressions that seem significant. Take whatever comes as a gift from God and turn it back to him in the form of a prayer. Thank him for his incarnation and invite him to be with you in a special way this Christmas.

Pray:

Moonless darkness stands between.
Past, the Past, no more be seen!
But the Bethlehem-star may lead me
to the sight of Him who freed me
from the self that I have been.
Make me pure, Lord: Thou art holy;
Make me meek, Lord: Thou wert lowly;
Now beginning, and alway:
Now begin, on Christmas day.

("Moonless Darkness" by Gerard Manley Hopkins)

Christmastide Day 2
DREW WILLIAMS

Read: *Luke 2:25–38*

Now there was a man in Jerusalem, whose name was Simeon, and this man was righteous and devout, waiting for the consolation of Israel, and the Holy Spirit was upon him. And it had been revealed to him by the Holy Spirit that he would not see death before he had seen the Lord's Christ. And he came in the Spirit into the temple, and when the parents brought in the child Jesus, to do for him according to the custom of the Law, he took him up in his arms and blessed God and said,

"Lord, now you are letting your servant depart in peace,
according to your word;
for my eyes have seen your salvation
that you have prepared in the presence of all peoples,
a light for revelation to the Gentiles,
and for glory to your people Israel."

And his father and his mother marveled at what was said about him. And Simeon blessed them and said to Mary his mother, "Behold, this child is appointed for the fall and rising of many in Israel, and for a sign that is opposed (and a sword will pierce through your own soul also), so that thoughts from many hearts may be revealed."

And there was a prophetess, Anna, the daughter of Phanuel, of the tribe of Asher. She was advanced in years, having lived with her husband seven years from when she was a virgin, and then as a widow until she was eighty-four. She did not depart from the temple, worshiping with fasting and prayer night and day. And coming up at that very hour she began to give thanks to God and to speak of him to all who were waiting for the redemption of Jerusalem.

Reflect:

Of all the people in the temple that day, why is it that Simeon and Anna were chosen to recognize the long-awaited Messiah in the arms of a young mother? We might imagine it was because they both had attained some extra measure of personal piety. Luke described Simeon as righteous and devout. Anna virtually lived at the temple, worshipping God with fasting and prayer night and day. Luke was not suggesting, however, that these individuals were without sin. In the book of Psalms, the righteous were certainly not without sin, as Psalm 32 teaches us. Rather, they were those who did not rest in their sin but repented and trusted God. In the Old Testament, the righteous were those who chose to make following God a way of life.

No doubt that Simeon and Anna were both remarkably faithful people, but something else distinguished them in their cloistered encounter with the infant Jesus. The clue is in Luke's description of Simeon: "The Holy Spirit was upon him" (v. 25). It was the gift of the Holy Spirit that had stirred in them both such a longing for the fulfillment of the presence and promise of Jesus. We discover that same longing and that same gift in David, a man who was not without fault but who nevertheless was a man after God's own heart. He was a man anointed by God's Spirit who would pray, "As the deer pants for streams of water, so my soul pants for you, my God" (Psalm 42:1 NIV).

Simeon and Anna shared this extraordinary and intimate audience with the infant Messiah because, even in their old age, they had not let the gift of the Spirit grow cold. The Holy Spirit longs to fill and stir up our hearts. He enables people in every generation to long for and recognize the presence and promise of Jesus. As you pray, ask God that you might desire more and more to know him, just as Simeon and Anna did.

Pray:

Holy Spirit, lift my heart and stir in me a longing for the presence and promise of Jesus. Amen.

Christmastide Day 3
DREW WILLIAMS

Read: *Matthew 2:13–15*

Now when they had departed, behold, an angel of the Lord appeared to Joseph in a dream and said, "Rise, take the child and his mother, and flee to Egypt, and remain there until I tell you, for Herod is about to search for the child, to destroy him." And he rose and took the child and his mother by night and departed to Egypt and remained there until the death of Herod. This was to fulfill what the Lord had spoken by the prophet, "Out of Egypt I called my son."

Reflect:

Leading up to this warning to flee to Egypt, Joseph had found himself being severely tested and challenged. He had known the deepest betrayal of the heart; he had suffered broken hopes and the pain of a lost future—laced with the poison of public humiliation. Mary and Joseph's betrothal was a binding agreement, and it gave Joseph legal remedies for Mary's apparent betrayal. He had the prerogative to publicly divorce Mary on the grounds of adultery, claim the dowry, and have her stoned to death.

But he didn't publicly clear his name, or receive a little financial restitution for his trouble, or dispose of the infamy of Mary's continuing presence in the community. Mary's and the infant Jesus's safety lay within Joseph's hands. He stayed with Mary. The baby had been born and now God asked yet another thing. Move to Egypt. In the crucible of his losses, he clung to the character and tender mercy of God.

Had Joseph held on to his anger or the sense that he had already "done enough," would he have received this second dream? Would he have had the heart to hear and respond to this new critical prophetic warning to take the infant Jesus and Mary to safety in Egypt? It was the mercy of God that again helped him to recognize God's voice and plan. Living into mercy tunes our hearts to the frequency of God's own heart.

As you pray, ponder what you personally know about receiving and offering mercy. In what ways do you long for your Father to make you more like Jesus?

Pray:

Lord Jesus, in your great mercy, help me to recognize your voice and your plan. Let your mercy retune my heart to the frequency of your love. Amen.

Christmastide Day 4
DREW WILLIAMS

Read: *Matthew 2:16–23*

Then Herod, when he saw that he had been tricked by the wise men, became furious, and he sent and killed all the male children in Bethlehem and in all that region who were two years old or under, according to the time that he had ascertained from the wise men. Then was fulfilled what was spoken by the prophet Jeremiah:

"A voice was heard in Ramah,
> weeping and loud lamentation,
Rachel weeping for her children;
>> she refused to be comforted, because they are no more."

But when Herod died, behold, an angel of the Lord appeared in a dream to Joseph in Egypt, saying, "Rise, take the child and his mother and go to the land of Israel, for those who sought the child's life are dead." And he rose and took the child and his mother and went to the land of Israel. But when he heard that Archelaus was reigning over Judea in place of his father Herod, he was afraid to go there, and being warned in a dream he withdrew to the district of Galilee. And he went and lived in a city called Nazareth, so that what was spoken by the prophets might be fulfilled, that he would be called a Nazarene.

Reflect:

Joseph's life was wildly different from anything he might have imagined when he was first betrothed to Mary. And yet a series of extraordinary dreams brought Joseph into God's greater plan. In yesterday's passage, Joseph accepted God's plan and took a full and active part in it. Acting upon the instructions from his dream, Joseph took Mary and the infant Jesus to safety in Egypt.

Today's verses involve a dream that layed out a carefully timed set of prophetic instructions, plotting the course for Joseph to bring Jesus safely to Nazareth (via Egypt), narrowly avoiding Herod Archelaus.

Immediately, Joseph responded. He shepherded his family back to Nazareth and stood by Mary as a faithful husband and by Jesus as a faithful earthly father.

This sequence of prophetic instructions was not, however, the only thing that Joseph received from God. Out of this prophetic awakening, Joseph was blessed with a wholehearted trust and confidence that God would supply him with all the strength he needed to walk out his calling.

Sometimes our dilemma is not that we don't know what God is asking of us but whether or not we have the strength to walk it out. Do we ever have it in us to go through with what God is asking of us? The answer is invariably "Absolutely not!" And yet, as God was faithful to Joseph, so he is faithful to supply us with all the strength we need to wholeheartedly take up our part in his good plans. "The one who calls us you is faithful, and he will do it" (1 Thessalonians 5:24 NIV).

Pray for the willingness to receive the Spirit's power and presence so that you can live in obedience to his call on your life.

Pray:

Father, I thank you that in everything you call me to, you are faithful to supply the strength I need. This day, I ask you to fortify me in your love and mercy so that I may wholeheartedly take up the place that you have made for me in your good plans. Amen.

Christmastide Day 5
DREW WILLIAMS

Read: *Luke 2:41–52*

> Now his parents went to Jerusalem every year at the Feast of the
> Passover. And when he was twelve years old, they went up according
> to custom. And when the feast was ended, as they were returning,
> the boy Jesus stayed behind in Jerusalem. His parents did not know
> it, but supposing him to be in the group they went a day's journey,
> but then they began to search for him among their relatives and
> acquaintances, and when they did not find him, they returned to
> Jerusalem, searching for him. After three days they found him in
> the temple, sitting among the teachers, listening to them and asking
> them questions. And all who heard him were amazed at his under-
> standing and his answers. And when his parents saw him, they were
> astonished. And his mother said to him, "Son, why have you treated
> us so? Behold, your father and I have been searching for you in great
> distress." And he said to them, "Why were you looking for me?
> Did you not know that I must be in my Father's house?" And they
> did not understand the saying that he spoke to them. And he went
> down with them and came to Nazareth and was submissive to them.
> And his mother treasured up all these things in her heart.
>
> And Jesus increased in wisdom and in stature and in favor with
> God and man.

Reflect:

The twelfth year in the life of a Jewish boy was the final year of preparation before he entered fully into the religious life of the synagogue. We can
presume that Joseph would have taught the young Jesus the commandments
of the law and then, at twelve years of age, Jesus would have gone through a
ceremony by which he became a *bar mitzvah*, or "son of the commandment."
And this was the year Jesus chose to stay behind in the temple.

It is worth noting Jesus's strategy for learning. He intentionally sought
out teachers, and when he had identified them, he sat in their midst; Jesus

listened to their teaching, asked questions, and gave answers. Do we bring the same wholehearted attention to our heavenly Father's desire that we grow in the grace and knowledge of our Lord and Savior Jesus Christ?

There is profound mystery in our faith. Our ways are not God's ways, and there are matters that are truly beyond our comprehension. There is, however, much that the Lord has blessed us to understand. At just twelve years of age, Jesus demonstrated God's desire that we continually seek to grow in the knowledge and love of God.

Jesus also signaled that theological and spiritual formation is meant to take place in the heart of the community of God's people. Mary and Joseph did not find Jesus sitting alone behind a pillar, poring over ancient scrolls. They found him at the temple, in the very midst of those who could teach. He was listening and actively participating in a shared time of learning.

Pray about your own desires for your community of Christians. Will you ask the Lord to stir in your heart the same quest for understanding? Will you ask the Lord to give you the courage to take Jesus's example and seek to grow in the knowledge and love of God in the community of his people?

Pray:

Lord Jesus, stir in my heart a desire to grow in deeper knowledge and love of you. I ask that you also supply the courage to allow me to grow in understanding in the community of your people. Amen.

Christmastide Day 6
MADISON PERRY

Read: *Matthew 3:13–17*

> Then Jesus came from Galilee to the Jordan to John, to be baptized by him. John would have prevented him, saying, "I need to be baptized by you, and do you come to me?" But Jesus answered him, "Let it be so now, for thus it is fitting for us to fulfill all righteousness." Then he consented. And when Jesus was baptized, immediately he went up from the water, and behold, the heavens were opened to him, and he saw the Spirit of God descending like a dove and coming to rest on him; and behold, a voice from heaven said, "This is my beloved Son, with whom I am well pleased."

Reflect:

In Matthew's telling of Jesus's life, before Jesus became a public figure, expectations abounded that God was returning for his people. This return would be a time of great excitement, prosperity, and judgment. God's kingdom was coming; with it would come wrath for the disobedient but flourishing and joy for those who had repented. "Repent, for the kingdom of heaven is at hand," John the Baptist had announced (Matthew 3:2).

Out of the many who approached John seeking baptism, we know the name of only one. Jesus, an outsider without status from the hinterlands, did not seek repentance. Guided by the Holy Spirit, John discerned that Jesus had the stature of a holy man and that Jesus should baptize him instead. But Jesus insisted: "Thus it is fitting for us to fulfill all righteousness."

This tells us something about what it means for Jesus to be God and man. We may have heard that in the incarnation, God took on flesh, but this no mere matter of dress-up. The incarnation is God on display over the course of a human life. In Jesus, God lived a human life, showing us what the characteristics of humility and meekness look like. Jesus's righteousness is not simply blamelessness. Jesus's righteousness accepts every opportunity to surrender to the Father.

Jesus emerged from the water and the full miracle crystallized: "This is my beloved Son, with whom I am well pleased." Our lives are far from the righteousness of God, yet in Jesus we see that his faithfulness is *for us* and counts for us. Jesus repented on our behalf and draws us near to his Father.

Today is a day to lay down the stories we have tried to write for ourselves and to thank God that Jesus's life is our own. We are undeserving, yet God's love is boundless and unabated. His love for us couldn't be any stronger, exceeding death and lifting us up into his righteous goodness.

Pray:

Gracious Father, we renounce Satan and all the spiritual forces of wickedness that rebel against you. We renounce the evil powers of this world that corrupt and destroy your creatures. We renounce all sinful desires that draw us away from your love. We turn again to Jesus as our Savior, we trust in his grace and love, and we commit to follow and obey him as our Lord. In his precious name. Amen.

Christmastide Day 7
SALLY BREEDLOVE

Read: *Psalm 91:1–12, 15–16*

He who dwells in the shelter of the Most High
    will abide in the shadow of the Almighty.
I will say to the LORD, "My refuge and my fortress,
    my God, in whom I trust."
For he will deliver you from the snare of the fowler
    and from the deadly pestilence.
He will cover you with his pinions,
    and under his wings you will find refuge;
    his faithfulness is a shield and buckler.
You will not fear the terror of the night,
    nor the arrow that flies by day,
nor the pestilence that stalks in darkness,
    nor the destruction that wastes at noonday.
A thousand may fall at your side,
    ten thousand at your right hand,
    but it will not come near you.
You will only look with your eyes
    and see the recompense of the wicked.
Because you have made the LORD your dwelling place—
    the Most High, who is my refuge—
no evil shall be allowed to befall you,
    no plague come near your tent.
For he will command his angels concerning you
    to guard you in all your ways.
On their hands they will bear you up,
    lest you strike your foot against a stone....
"When he calls to me, I will answer him;
    I will be with him in trouble;
    I will rescue him and honor him.
With long life I will satisfy him
and show him my salvation."

Reflect:

For centuries, this psalm has been beloved by the church. It encompasses it all—full protection from everything, and the invitation to sink your life into the shelter and love of God. Perhaps the psalm leaves you comforted yet also with questions. It is deeply reassuring to know you are kept by the mighty and very present God. At the same time, perhaps you sense some resistance and questioning inside your soul. *No plagues? No evil? No pestilence? No fear?*

It's this psalm that the evil one quoted when he tempted Jesus to jump from the pinnacle of the temple so as to prove that God keeps his people from all harm all the time. But Jesus refused to turn the psalm into a proof text of God's goodness. Jesus, who fully feared, loved, and obeyed God, also endured a great deal of opposition in his life and ultimately died on the cross.

We long to know God as Christ did. We long to dwell beneath the shelter of his wings. We believe he is mighty and loving, but still, there is so much wrong and so many broken and scary things. Especially now.

It is New Year's Eve. A new year begins tomorrow morning. What will it be like? As you pray, pause and tell the truth about your own heart as you sit in this moment. Will you trust yourself to God's sheltering presence like Jesus did? Will you by faith believe that this beloved psalm speaks of the absolute and final outcome of our broken world? One day there will be no evil, no pestilence, no pain, no dying. Will you even now, in the midst of trouble, entrust your soul and the lives of those you love to the eternal God? He is your home and your strong shelter.

Think of people you know who are fearful and struggling. Pray they will know that God is their mighty shelter and that one day all will be made well.

Pray:

Father, we live in a land of disorder and pain. Yet we run to you for shelter, God Most High. Please grant us your rest. Let us know your Holy Spirit's peace, by which you led Paul and Silas to sing while in prison. Let us hear you singing over us as we sleep. Amen.

Christmastide Day 8
DREW WILLIAMS

Read: *Luke 4:1–13*

And Jesus, full of the Holy Spirit, returned from the Jordan and was
led by the Spirit in the wilderness for forty days, being tempted by
the devil. And he ate nothing during those days. And when they
were ended, he was hungry. The devil said to him, "If you are the
Son of God, command this stone to become bread." And Jesus
answered him, "It is written, 'Man shall not live by bread alone.'"
And the devil took him up and showed him all the kingdoms of the
world in a moment of time, and said to him, "To you I will give all
this authority and their glory, for it has been delivered to me, and
I give it to whom I will. If you, then, will worship me, it will all be
yours." And Jesus answered him, "It is written,

"'You shall worship the Lord your God,
and him only shall you serve.'"

And he took him to Jerusalem and set him on the pinnacle of the
temple and said to him, "If you are the Son of God, throw yourself
down from here, for it is written,

"'He will command his angels concerning you,
to guard you,' and "'On their hands they will bear you up,
lest you strike your foot against a stone.'"

And Jesus answered him, "It is said, 'You shall not put the Lord your
God to the test.'" And when the devil had ended every temptation,
he departed from him until an opportune time.

Reflect:

Jesus's resistance to the enemy in this desert battle had a lot riding on it.
Should Jesus succumb to the enemy's stratagem, then he would be proven
no better than the first Adam, causing the story of our salvation to end here.
Jesus's success in this moment of fierce combat ultimately led to his final
victory for us upon the cross. At the cross, Jesus disarmed the rulers and
authorities and put them to shame by triumphing over them. To fail in this
wilderness testing would have been to forfeit that ultimate victory.

In addition to the cosmic implications of this desert battle, the fact that the enemy's present-day strategy remains largely unaltered is also noteworthy. To Jesus in the desert and to us today, the enemy makes the same play. Does this sound remotely familiar: "Surely if you are a child of the King, then claim your blessings! God has promised to send you all manner of provisions to make you healthy, wealthy, and prosperous. Are you sure that you have what is truly owed to you?"

But Jesus did overcome the enemy in the desert, and his victory upon the cross is eternal and irrevocable. This means that while the enemy is stuck with the same old script, we have a new heart and a new spirit. The enemy still insinuates his tired propaganda, but we who wait for the Lord will renew our strength. The enemy attacks us from a place of defeat.

In Christ's victory we have been given authority over all the power of the enemy. The Holy Spirit will not let us be tempted beyond what we can bear. And Jesus has promised to provide a way out (1 Corinthians 10:13) so that we can endure. The enemy's propaganda might well remain the same, but in Jesus, the fierceness of the spiritual battle we are fighting has been radically changed in our present and eternal favor.

As you pray, pray for yourself in the arenas of your life where it is hard for you to stand firm in Jesus. Pray for God's mercy and help for those you know who are struggling.

Pray:

Lord Jesus, I stand on your victory on the cross. I now take my stand against Satan and all his lying ways and command him to depart from me. I put on the full armor of God so that I may be able to stand firm against all the strategies of the evil one. Amen.

Christmastide Day 9
STEVEN A. BREEDLOVE

Read: *John 1:1–5, 14, 16–18*

In the beginning was the Word, and the Word was with God, and the Word was God. He was in the beginning with God. All things were made through him, and without him was not any thing made that was made. In him was life, and the life was the light of men. The light shines in the darkness, and the darkness has not overcome it....

And the Word became flesh and dwelt among us, and we have seen his glory, glory as of the only Son from the Father, full of grace and truth.... For from his fullness we have all received, grace upon grace. For the law was given through Moses; grace and truth came through Jesus Christ. No one has ever seen God; the only God, who is at the Father's side, he has made him known.

Reflect:

John began his Gospel by pulling back the curtain on the mysteries of the essential identity and nature of God. He invited us into an unfamiliar world to hear words that human faculties are not strong enough to fully understand. We see from afar. This is holy ground.

Don't turn away quickly from mystery. Take off your shoes and stay awhile. At the least, we can absorb this: From before time, the God we never fully understand is communicating. He is the Word, eternally reaching out, making himself known. He is Life, begetting life. He is Light, bringing forth light so that darkness must loosen its grip on us. Life and light will grow if we'll only linger and look.

Not content to dwell in mysteries beyond our ken, the Word became flesh and dwelt among us. Later John wrote, "That which was from the beginning, which we have heard, which we have seen with our eyes, which we have looked at and our hands have touched—this we proclaim concerning the Word of life" (1 John 1:1 NIV).

John's Gospel burden is for us to know that when we see Jesus, we see God. When we learn something from Jesus, the Light that is Life itself is shining. The eternal Word, Creator God, became a person we could see, talk with, touch, handle. Jesus has made the God we can never see understandable and knowable. We can say we know God because we see Jesus. Amazing love. How can it be?

Later, Jesus invited two curious disciples of John the Baptist to come to his house. His words were simple: "Come and see." And they did as he had bid. Indications are that they sat and talked with him for hours through the evening meal. The passion of God to personally connect with people bridged the gap from the unfathomable mysteries of eternity to the simple homeliness of a kitchen table in ancient Israel.

How much does God want to communicate with you? How much does he want you to know him, to be his familiar friend?

As you pray, ask God to give you the determination to sit with Jesus, to linger with him, to talk with him, and to listen to him. That's what he wants, any and every day and night, for the rest of your life.

Pray:

Heavenly Father, give me a heart that longs to linger in your presence. Amen.

Christmastide Day 10
STEVEN A. BREEDLOVE

Read: *John 2:13–22*

The Passover of the Jews was at hand, and Jesus went up to Jerusalem. In the temple he found those who were selling oxen and sheep and pigeons, and the money-changers sitting there. And making a whip of cords, he drove them all out of the temple, with the sheep and oxen. And he poured out the coins of the money-changers and overturned their tables. And he told those who sold the pigeons, "Take these things away; do not make my Father's house a house of trade." His disciples remembered that it was written, "Zeal for your house will consume me."

So the Jews said to him, "What sign do you show us for doing these things?" Jesus answered them, "Destroy this temple, and in three days I will raise it up." The Jews then said, "It has taken forty-six years to build this temple, and will you raise it up in three days?" But he was speaking about the temple of his body. When therefore he was raised from the dead, his disciples remembered that he had said this, and they believed the Scripture and the word that Jesus had spoken.

Reflect:

Invariably, the question emerges: "One cleansing of the temple or two?" A good case can be made for either, but surely it is no stretch of the imagination to see that money changers and marketers could have quickly reverted to their greedy ways as soon as the pressure let up. Don't we do the same with our fond sins?

However, as you turn to consider the actual event, keep in mind that Jesus has made the God we can never see understandable and knowable. "No one has ever seen God, but the one and only Son, who is himself God and is in closest relationship with the Father, has made him known" (John 1:18 NIV). When Jesus cleansed the temple of the tools of marketing and banking, God was acting. The Word was speaking. Light was invading darkness. Life was making its presence known.

The message that God declared reveals his priority for dedicated space (and time) when we are not occupied with the cares of this world, when we can focus, listen, reflect, pray, and draw near to him. Silencing distractions is not just for serious followers. This housecleaning occurred in the court of the Gentiles, space set aside for "outsiders" to approach God in order to listen, learn, and pray in their own quests for truth. Dozens of languages could have theoretically been heard there every day, but God's message was singular and understandable for any ears: "I prioritize devotion and worship! Therefore, you must prioritize devotion and worship." Jesus was righteously angry when he declared this message by his actions, but the Word was turning on a light in our darkness. We are being pushed toward life.

One of the fiercest battles in our lifelong journey of following Christ is accepting the fact that he sets the terms. He does, and his terms are clear: "I want your attention and your heart!"

As you begin your time of prayer, consider your own soul in this season. Has Jesus forcibly scattered your well-organized, meticulously counted coins in the dirt? Has he gotten your attention? If so, then why go back to the way it was? Why not take his message to heart? How can you maintain God's own priority, a time when distractions are laid aside in favor of focused listening, prayer, and reflection?

Pray:

Gracious and holy Father, please give me intellect to understand you, reason to discern you, diligence to seek you, wisdom to find you, a spirit to know you, a heart to meditate upon you, ears to hear you, eyes to see you, a tongue to proclaim you, a way of life pleasing to you, patience to wait for you, and perseverance to look for you. Grant me a perfect end, your holy presence, a blessed resurrection, and life everlasting. Amen.

(Benedict of Nursia)

Christmastide Day 11
STEVEN A. BREEDLOVE

Read: *John 3:1–10*

Now there was a man of the Pharisees named Nicodemus, a ruler of the Jews. This man came to Jesus by night and said to him, "Rabbi, we know that you are a teacher come from God, for no one can do these signs that you do unless God is with him." Jesus answered him, "Truly, truly, I say to you, unless one is born again he cannot see the kingdom of God."

Nicodemus said to him, "How can a man be born when he is old? Can he enter a second time into his mother's womb and be born?" Jesus answered, "Truly, truly, I say to you, unless one is born of water and the Spirit, he cannot enter the kingdom of God. That which is born of the flesh is flesh, and that which is born of the Spirit is spirit. Do not marvel that I said to you, 'You must be born again.' The wind blows where it wishes, and you hear its sound, but you do not know where it comes from or where it goes. So it is with everyone who is born of the Spirit."

Nicodemus said to him, "How can these things be?" Jesus answered him, "Are you the teacher of Israel and yet you do not understand these things?"

Reflect:

Have you been born? Yes or no? Do you know for sure? Have you given birth? Do you know for sure? Ridiculous questions! We know we have been born. We know whether we have given birth. Birth and giving birth are definitive markers as obvious as the ground beneath our feet.

Jesus says that the second birth is just as definitive. Unfortunately, many of us struggle at times to know for sure whether we are born again or whether being born again is a certain reality. The apostles Peter and Paul help us here.

Peter wrote declaratively in 1 Peter 1:3, "Blessed be the God and Father of our Lord Jesus Christ! According to his great mercy, he has caused us to be born again to a living hope through the resurrection of Jesus Christ from the dead." In Christ, we have been born again! Peter went on to declare that this new life breathes the air of hope, acts by tested faith, and grows in love.

As we dig deeper, we realize that this declaration of the nature of new life is also an invitation, an aspiration, and a decision. *We live into what we are declared to be, taking on the shape of the life that God has already drawn for us in Christ.* Paul said it even more pointedly in Philippians 3:12: "I press on to make it my own [i.e., a life of knowing Christ], because Christ Jesus has made me his own." Paul was saying, *Jesus has given me a certain kind of life. I choose this life, pressing on toward the goal, the prize.*

The question, then, is quite simple: Do you want to be born again? Are you hopeful that Christ will give you eternal life? Do you long for that life? If so, then by definition, he has already implanted new life in you. The Spirit is at work. Hold tight to the hand that is already holding you tight!

As you pray, consider one promise you've been given in Christ and receive it as sure hope. Think of the first thing that you know God has told you to do (or not to do), and then do it (or stop doing it). Aspire to love Jesus and others whom he is calling you to love. Write down or speak aloud your hope, faith, and love.

Pray:

Grant me, even me, my dearest Lord, to know you, and love you, and rejoice in you. And, if I cannot do these perfectly in this life, let me at least advance to higher degrees every day, until I can come to do them in perfection. Let the knowledge of you increase in me here, that it may be full hereafter. Let the love of you grow every day more and more here, that it may be perfect hereafter; that my joy may be full in you. Amen.

(Saint Augustine)

Christmastide Day 12
STEVEN A. BREEDLOVE

Read: *John 3:25–36*

> Now a discussion arose between some of John's disciples and a Jew over purification. And they came to John and said to him, "Rabbi, he who was with you across the Jordan, to whom you bore witness— look, he is baptizing, and all are going to him." John answered, "A person cannot receive even one thing unless it is given him from heaven. You yourselves bear me witness, that I said, 'I am not the Christ, but I have been sent before him.' The one who has the bride is the bridegroom. The friend of the bridegroom, who stands and hears him, rejoices greatly at the bridegroom's voice. Therefore this joy of mine is now complete. He must increase, but I must decrease."
>
> He who comes from above is above all. He who is of the earth belongs to the earth and speaks in an earthly way. He who comes from heaven is above all. He bears witness to what he has seen and heard, yet no one receives his testimony. Whoever receives his testimony sets his seal to this, that God is true. For he whom God has sent utters the words of God, for he gives the Spirit without measure. The Father loves the Son and has given all things into his hand. Whoever believes in the Son has eternal life; whoever does not obey the Son shall not see life, but the wrath of God remains on him.

Reflect:

John's goal was to present Jesus as "the Christ, the Son of God," and to convince us to believe in Christ and "have life in his name" (John 20:30–31). Such an emphasis should give us a measure of holy discomfort. We love John 15:15: "No longer do I call you servants . . . but I have called you friends." We run when he invites, "Come to me, all who labor" (Matthew 11:28). But this same Jesus also cleansed the temple with a whip in John 2. He confronted Nicodemus bluntly: "Unless one is born again he cannot see the kingdom of God" (John 3:3). Christ pulls no punches.

John the Baptist was an exemplary disciple of the Lord; he established a governing GPS signal for the Christian life: "He must increase, but I must decrease. He who comes from above is above all" (John 3:30–31). In this posture of submissive allegiance, John said, "This joy of mine is now complete" (John 3:29).

In order for Jesus to increase, he must do so in two seemingly discordant directions. He must increase as Commander. Are we willing to welcome Jesus as "above all"? Will we accept the terms he sets, or do we imbibe the spirit of our world, sitting in judgment of Jesus, determining whether or not what he says fits our sensibilities and logic?

But he must also increase as the one who comes from heaven to earth, to us. He tells us what he has seen and heard about a world infinitely truer and more beautiful than what we can imagine. He offers to us his own first and best gift—his Spirit—without measure.

How do we hold together "Commander" and "Comer"? Be assured, he is always both.

As you pray, consciously consider Jesus the Christ. Ask him how he might increase in stature in your soul and imagination, and how you might decrease in your need for recognition and satisfaction. Welcome him in your prayers. Rest. Rejoice. Receive.

Pray:

Lord Jesus Christ, I am no longer my own, but thine. Put me to what thou wilt, rank me with whom thou wilt. Put me to doing, put me to suffering. Let me be employed by thee or laid aside for thee, exalted for thee or brought low for thee. Let me be full, let me be empty. Let me have all things, let me have nothing. I freely and heartily yield all things to thy pleasure and disposal. And now, O glorious and blessed God, Father, Son, and Holy Spirit, thou are mine, and I am thine. So be it. And the covenant which I have made on earth, let it be ratified in heaven. Amen.

(John Wesley)

Introduction to Epiphany

STEVEN E. BREEDLOVE

*T*HE WORD *EPIPHANY* MEANS "MANIFESTATION," and the Feast of Epiphany, celebrated on January 6, commemorates the manifestation of Jesus Christ to the Magi, who represent the entire Gentile world.

This is a feast day in the life of the church because it commemorates that God revealed himself not just to the people of Israel but also to those outside the promise. The Magi were the first, but the Gospels record Jesus's interactions with other Gentiles, and the book of Acts demonstrates God's plan to bring salvation in the name of Jesus to every tribe, tongue, and nation. Most of us are, by God's grace, recipients of this kindness, so we celebrate the fact that the doors of salvation are open wide to those not numbered among the Israelites!

The season of Epiphany follows the feast day. During this season, we are given the chance to focus on who God has revealed himself to be in Jesus Christ. We are encouraged to celebrate not just a general revelation of his existence but also the specific manifestation of the character of Jesus Christ, who is God in the flesh. The Magi worshipped him as King, though they were kneeling before a humble child. Do we see the nature of Jesus as clearly as they?

Prayer during Epiphany springs from the desire to understand Jesus Christ. Rather than emphasizing application or obedience, our devotional readings focus on simply seeing Jesus clearly. In this season, we pray that God will reveal himself to us as we read and that we hunger to understand the character of our Lord Jesus Christ, because in him, Father, Son, and Holy Spirit are made manifest!

Epiphany Day 1
STEVEN A. BREEDLOVE

Read: *Matthew 2:1–2, 11–12*

Now after Jesus was born in Bethlehem of Judea in the days of Herod the king, behold, wise men from the east came to Jerusalem, saying, "Where is he who has been born king of the Jews? For we saw his star when it rose and have come to worship him."...

And going into the house, they saw the child with Mary his mother, and they fell down and worshiped him. Then, opening their treasures, they offered him gifts, gold and frankincense and myrrh. And being warned in a dream not to return to Herod, they departed to their own country by another way.

Reflect:

Who attended Jesus's birth? Who witnessed the coming of the Son of God? His mother and earthly father, "blue collar" shepherds, a host of angels, and the Magi.

Who attended the death of Jesus? Again, his mother, plus a different set of blue-collar people, his disciples. There were also angels, alert and waiting, while the mystery of redemption unfolded. Politicians and religious leaders united to eliminate the threat of a supposed king. And there were two wealthy wise men, Joseph of Arimathea and Nicodemus.

Isn't it fascinating that the two milestones in the human life of the Son of God, his birth and death, were attended by everyday people plus some unusually wealthy, learned people? Why would the Father guide wealthy men to both the crib and the cross?

Maybe there's a message of comfort here. While it may be difficult for a wealthy ("learned") person to enter the kingdom of God, it is not impossible (Mark 10:23–27). But perhaps another reason is that the Father simply wanted to honor his Son. After the unthinkable injustice, pain, and shame of the cross, perhaps the Father wanted to make a statement. He stirred up

Joseph and Nicodemus, two men who had come to hope in Jesus as Messiah, to beautify his brutalized body with a rich man's burial.

Perhaps the same tenderness filters into the story of the Magi. Yes, there are primary messages about epiphany and gospel mission. But their worship also triggered one of Scripture's darkest stories of injustice, murder, and grief. The Son was born into a tragic, sinful, often ugly world. Perhaps these birth gifts from wealthy men were, among other things, a statement from a Father to his Son.

We normally mark births with gifts. We mark deaths with eulogies and gratitude, sometimes giving charitable gifts to honor the departed. Would it be so strange if the God of love were to mark both the birth and death of his Son with gifts of love?

As you pray, receive these words from the Beloved: "As the Father has loved me, so have I loved you" (John 15:9 NIV). Receive this assurance from the Holy Spirit: "Nothing in all creation will ever be able to separate us from the love of God that is revealed in Christ Jesus our Lord" (Romans 8:39 NLT).

Pray:

Look on us, O Lord, and let all the darkness of our souls vanish before the beams of your brightness. Fill us with holy love, and open to us the treasures of your wisdom. All our desires are known to you, therefore complete what you have begun, and what your Spirit has awakened us to ask in prayer. We seek your face, turn your face to us and show us your glory. Then will our longing be satisfied, and our peace shall be perfect. Amen.

(Saint Augustine)

Epiphany Day 2
FRANCIS CAPITANIO

Read: *John 4:5–18, 27*

So he came to a town of Samaria called Sychar, near the field that Jacob had given to his son Joseph. Jacob's well was there; so Jesus, wearied as he was from his journey, was sitting beside the well. It was about the sixth hour.

A woman from Samaria came to draw water. Jesus said to her, "Give me a drink." (For his disciples had gone away into the city to buy food.) The Samaritan woman said to him, "How is it that you, a Jew, ask for a drink from me, a woman of Samaria?" (For Jews have no dealings with Samaritans.) Jesus answered her, "If you knew the gift of God, and who it is that is saying to you, 'Give me a drink,' you would have asked him, and he would have given you living water." The woman said to him, "Sir, you have nothing to draw water with, and the well is deep. Where do you get that living water? Are you greater than our father Jacob? He gave us the well and drank from it himself, as did his sons and his livestock." Jesus said to her, "Everyone who drinks of this water will be thirsty again, but whoever drinks of the water that I will give him will never be thirsty again. The water that I will give him will become in him a spring of water welling up to eternal life." The woman said to him, "Sir, give me this water, so that I will not be thirsty or have to come here to draw water."

Jesus said to her, "Go, call your husband, and come here." The woman answered him, "I have no husband." Jesus said to her, "You are right in saying, 'I have no husband'; for you have had five husbands, and the one you now have is not your husband. What you have said is true."…

Just then his disciples came back. They marveled that he was talking with a woman, but no one said, "What do you seek?" or, "Why are you talking with her?"

Reflect:

Have you ever been surprised to find that Jesus is talking with you? If so, then you may see yourself in the Samaritan woman. She was looked down on by God's people and Christ's disciples, and though the Twelve would not admit it, they couldn't grasp why Jesus would condescend to speak to a Samaritan, a woman, and a sinner. There are many voices within each of us that think the same thing when we come to the Lord to pray. They argue, "But Jesus, don't you know who it is you're talking to?"

We see our own unworthiness to come before the Son of God, yet this can cause us to see the greatness of his love with even greater clarity. The same one who condescended to speak to Moses from the cloud and the pillar of fire spoke to the Samaritan woman and meets with each one of us. This shows the greatness of his humility; there is nothing equal to his lowliness. Jesus made lowliness and meekness the foundation of all he had to say in the Beatitudes. We see this humility perfectly in Jesus as he conversed with a simple, sinful woman who was eager to hear about the kingdom of God.

As we pray, let us all remember that we are no better than the Samaritan woman, yet he longs to be with us still. When we consider our weaknesses, the unsteadiness of our will, our inner pride, and the multitude of our sins, we should see his greatness, even as we see his love, because he wants to be right where we are. He knows us and he still wants us. The Samaritan woman was in good company sitting by the well, conversing with the Lord. We can sit there too.

Pray:

Lord, I don't know why you want to talk with me, but I know that you do. As the voices within me rise up to condemn me, quiet them with your love, and let them know that you are here to give me living water despite where I've been and who I am. I am thirsty. Thank you for letting that be enough. Amen.

Epiphany Day 3
FRANCIS CAPITANIO

Read: *John 4:43–54*

After the two days he departed for Galilee. (For Jesus himself had testified that a prophet has no honor in his own hometown.) So when he came to Galilee, the Galileans welcomed him, having seen all that he had done in Jerusalem at the feast. For they too had gone to the feast.

So he came again to Cana in Galilee, where he had made the water wine. And at Capernaum there was an official whose son was ill. When this man heard that Jesus had come from Judea to Galilee, he went to him and asked him to come down and heal his son, for he was at the point of death. So Jesus said to him, "Unless you see signs and wonders you will not believe." The official said to him, "Sir, come down before my child dies." Jesus said to him, "Go; your son will live." The man believed the word that Jesus spoke to him and went on his way. As he was going down, his servants met him and told him that his son was recovering. So he asked them the hour when he began to get better, and they said to him, "Yesterday at the seventh hour the fever left him." The father knew that was the hour when Jesus had said to him, "Your son will live." And he himself believed, and all his household. This was now the second sign that Jesus did when he had come from Judea to Galilee.

Reflect:

The New International Version says, "The man took Jesus at his word and departed" (John 4:50 NIV).

When we come to the Lord in prayer, do we ask him for what we need with confidence? Do we believe that he will do what is best for us and that, having asked, we have put our needs in his capable hands? Do we depart in peace?

Or, on the contrary, do we hold on to our anxiety? Do we get angry because we feel he is cheating us of what we deserve? Do we demand a sign so that we know he will do what we ask?

Like the royal official who asked Jesus to heal his son, we should strive to take Jesus at his word and depart to go on with our day with the confidence that he knows our needs and will meet them. It seems that Jesus rebuked the crowd by saying, "Unless you see signs and wonders you will not believe" (v. 48). And yet he performed the sign for this man, who then believed, along with his whole household.

Sometimes, because of our weaknesses, we need a sign to believe, and God is willing to give it. Sometimes we don't need a sign or God isn't willing to give one. But at the core of all our requests, we must believe that Jesus knows what we need, whether his answer is a yes or a no to whatever it is we ask.

Prayer meets trust at the moment we depart. It's at this point, when we walk away to continue with our day, that true faith is tested and refined if we take him at his word.

As you pray, ask for the faith to take Jesus at his word.

Pray:

Lord Jesus Christ, as I leave my prayers and the reading of Scripture behind in order to begin my day, I know you don't leave me behind. As I depart from prayer, you do not depart from me. But as I go about my day, give me the faith to know that you have heard my requests, that you love me, and that you know what I need when I need it. Knowing all this, let me depart in peace to do the work you have given me to do this day. Amen.

Epiphany Day 4
KARI WEST

Read: *Psalm 70*

> Make haste, O God, to deliver me!
>   O LORD, make haste to help me!
> Let them be put to shame and confusion
>   who seek my life!
> Let them be turned back and brought to dishonor
>   who delight in my hurt!
> Let them turn back because of their shame
>   who say, "Aha, Aha!"
> May all who seek you
>   rejoice and be glad in you!
> May those who love your salvation
>   say evermore, "God is great!"
> But I am poor and needy;
>   hasten to me, O God!
> You are my help and my deliverer;
>   O LORD, do not delay!

Reflect:

Do you turn to the Lord in desperate times? Do you offer quick prayers—like gasps, like cries for help—to your God? David was assailed on all sides. He faced enemies who jeered at him, mocked him, sought his ruin—and some who even sought to take his life. In his terror, poverty, and neediness, he begged the Lord for succor.

How we need God's help to know our own insufficiency in hardships. How quickly we grasp for our false saviors. Maybe we turn inward, assuming that if we just dwell on our problems long enough, we can come up with our own solutions. Maybe we distract ourselves, reaching for comfort, or pleasure, or sleep to dull the difficulty. Maybe we take our rage and exhaustion out on those around us, enjoying the momentary relief and then enduring the lingering guilt.

Perhaps our greatest weakness is our self-deception, our persistence in the lie of self-sufficiency. We must learn to acknowledge, with David, that we are poor and needy and in desperate need of God's rescue.

The Holy Spirit is willing and ready to teach us.

As you pray, ask for what you need, starting with the need to know your own neediness. Ask the Holy Spirit to lead you into deeper humility and deeper peace. Praise Christ for his grace that bears us up in every circumstance.

Pray:

Almighty and everlasting God, you are always more ready to hear than we to pray, and to give more than we either desire or deserve: Pour down upon us the abundance of your mercy, forgiving us those things of which our conscience is afraid, and giving us those good things for which we are not worthy to ask, except through the merits and mediation of Jesus Christ our Savior; who lives and reigns with you and the Holy Spirit, one God, for ever and ever. Amen.

(Anglican Church in North America Book of Common Prayer)

Epiphany Day 5
KARI WEST

Read: *Genesis 1:1–5*

In the beginning, God created the heavens and the earth. The earth was without form and void, and darkness was over the face of the deep. And the Spirit of God was hovering over the face of the waters.

And God said, "Let there be light," and there was light. And God saw that the light was good. And God separated the light from the darkness. God called the light Day, and the darkness he called Night. And there was evening and there was morning, the first day.

Reflect:

God draws near to what is formless and empty. He hovers over it like a bird hovering and fluttering her wings over her nest, and he brings about life, newness, order, beauty.

This is the very first thing we ever learn about the Lord from Scripture: he is a God who creates. He is for life, for teeming, full-bodied, varied, glorious existence. He spoke light into reality. And what was the very first word that God used to describe what he had made? It was good.

God is still for what he has made by the word of his power. He is still a Creator, still speaking life into his world, though that world has fractured almost beyond recognition. Creation is still held together in Christ—for whom and by whom all things were made—and it will be remade by him.

Christ is that very good light for all humankind, shining in the darkness, never to be overcome.

As you pray, rest in God as the crafter of all that is good. Recall something lovely in the world and thank him for making it. Praise him for his word of power and his firm commitment to the good of his creation. Hope in the coming restoration of all things.

Pray:

O God, you made all things, and in you all things hold together. You are our Creator, and the world is full of your majesty and love. We praise you, our Father and our King. Your kingdom come and your will be done on earth as it is in heaven, we pray. Amen.

Epiphany Day 6
MADISON PERRY

Read: *Genesis 17:3–8; 22:17–18*

Then Abram fell on his face. And God said to him, "Behold, my covenant is with you, and you shall be the father of a multitude of nations. No longer shall your name be called Abram, but your name shall be Abraham, for I have made you the father of a multitude of nations. I will make you exceedingly fruitful, and I will make you into nations, and kings shall come from you. And I will establish my covenant between me and you and your offspring after you throughout their generations for an everlasting covenant, to be God to you and to your offspring after you. And I will give to you and to your offspring after you the land of your sojournings, all the land of Canaan, for an everlasting possession, and I will be their God."…

"I will surely bless you, and I will surely multiply your offspring as the stars of heaven and as the sand that is on the seashore. And your offspring shall possess the gate of his enemies, and in your offspring shall all the nations of the earth be blessed, because you have obeyed my voice."

Reflect:

Abram, the sojourner from ancient times, faced God in conversation and ended up on his face. He was on a journey with God, but where it would take him he did not know. God was still shaping him, naming him, and narrating his future.

Whatever today may hold, whatever possibilities for success and failure, pleasure and pain, this day bears a marvelous opportunity: to be in relationship with the God who loves us and wants to tell us what our future is in him.

Seeking God cast Abram on his face, but then God showed him what was to come. Abram would have a new name, Abraham. And the very best to come would not include building Abraham a palace for himself. No, he would remain a sojourner. But his life would lead to the very best of all outcomes. God would govern the world through Abraham's descendants, who would dwell in peace and the fullness of prosperity.

We come from dust and we are bound for dust, but if we know God and hold fast to his promises, these promises of Abraham extend to us. Our lives are limited, and our days are numbered. But God's promises are forever.

If you knew that God's greatest work through you would come to fruition only in future generations, who or what would you focus on today? Is it disappointing to think that you are not the center of the story? You remain in the center of God's sight, nonetheless. Praise him and receive his love.

Pray:

Our Lord of covenant faithfulness, let us rest in you. Thank you that you are our God throughout all generations. Glory be to you forever and ever. Amen.

Epiphany Day 7
KARI WEST

Read: *Exodus 3:7–12*

> Then the LORD said, "I have surely seen the affliction of my people who are in Egypt and have heard their cry because of their task-masters. I know their sufferings, and I have come down to deliver them out of the hand of the Egyptians and to bring them up out of that land to a good and broad land, a land flowing with milk and honey, to the place of the Canaanites, the Hittites, the Amorites, the Perizzites, the Hivites, and the Jebusites. And now, behold, the cry of the people of Israel has come to me, and I have also seen the oppression with which the Egyptians oppress them. Come, I will send you to Pharaoh that you may bring my people, the children of Israel, out of Egypt." But Moses said to God, "Who am I that I should go to Pharaoh and bring the children of Israel out of Egypt?" He said, "But I will be with you, and this shall be the sign for you, that I have sent you: when you have brought the people out of Egypt, you shall serve God on this mountain."

Reflect:

We serve an attentive, compassionate, powerful God. The Lord witnessed the afflictions of his people, was moved by their suffering, and worked to bring them out of slavery and into a good, spacious, abundant land.

Do you believe that God sees you and hears you? Do you know that he is full of compassion for you? We, too, have been rescued from slavery and are being led to good and spacious land, not through the fearful and uncertain Moses but by the perfect and obedient Christ.

Your hardships and your tears never go unnoticed by the Lord. He has wrought your greatest rescue, and he will keep you by his power until you are "planted on the mountain of his holy inheritance—the place made for his dwelling" (Exodus 15:17, author's paraphrase).

As you pray, confess what is hard in your life. Offer these difficulties to the Lord. Then read these verses again and ask for greater faith in our attentive, rescuing God. Know that he will always do good and he will act in his perfect timing. Rest in the saving work of Christ.

Pray:

"The LORD is my strength and my defense; he has become my salvation. He is my God, and I will praise him, my father's God, and I will exalt him." Amen.

(Exodus 15:2 NIV)

Epiphany Day 8
MADISON PERRY

Read: *Psalm 1*

> Blessed is the man
>> who walks not in the counsel of the wicked,
> nor stands in the way of sinners,
>> nor sits in the seat of scoffers;
> but his delight is in the law of the LORD,
>> and on his law he meditates day and night.
> He is like a tree
>> planted by streams of water
> that yields its fruit in its season,
>> and its leaf does not wither.
> In all that he does, he prospers.
> The wicked are not so,
>> but are like chaff that the wind drives away.
> Therefore the wicked will not stand in the judgment,
>> nor sinners in the congregation of the righteous;
> for the LORD knows the way of the righteous,
>> but the way of the wicked will perish.

Reflect:

Psalm 1 describes God's prototype for maturity. It speaks of a single righteous person who is like a tree. For Christians, that person is Jesus, who hung on a tree. From his life we receive a life that will look like his life, as will our growth.

The growth of a tree never makes the headlines. A tree's growth is slow and steady, unremarkable and repeated. Every day, trees draw water. Every evening, they stretch their limbs and shake their leaves.

Regardless of our circumstances, each day presents us with chances for newness and growth. We may prefer more radical periods of drastic motion, but in this picture the life of the Spirit patiently persists over time. Continue in regular prayer. Seek the Lord. Do the ordinary things you already know to do. Continue in this basic and organic God-given life, every day a resurrection.

It is sometimes said that the righteous person is simply the person who prays Psalm 1 and means it. As you pray, appreciate the life that flows into you from God's Vine, our Lord Jesus Christ. Feel your roots settle. Maybe lift your arms toward God's light. He is good and intends good for us. He sees farther than where we will be tomorrow. He sees a whole leafy forest of children and blessings he will bring about through our slow and steady submission.

Pray:
How well God must like you—
    you don't walk in the ruts of those blind-as-bats,
    you don't stand with the good-for-nothings,
    you don't take your seat among the know-it-alls.
Instead you thrill to GOD's Word,
    you chew on Scripture day and night.
You're a tree replanted in Eden,
    bearing fresh fruit every month,
Never dropping a leaf,
    always in blossom.
You're not at all like the wicked,
    who are mere windblown dust—
Without defense in court,
    unfit company for innocent people.
GOD charts the road you take.
    The road *they* take leads to nowhere.
Amen.

(Psalm 1 MSG)

Epiphany Day 9
KARI WEST

Read: *1 Samuel 16:4–13*

Samuel did what the LORD commanded and came to Bethlehem. The elders of the city came to meet him trembling and said, "Do you come peaceably?" And he said, "Peaceably; I have come to sacrifice to the LORD. Consecrate yourselves, and come with me to the sacrifice." And he consecrated Jesse and his sons and invited them to the sacrifice.

When they came, he looked on Eliab and thought, "Surely the LORD's anointed is before him." But the LORD said to Samuel, "Do not look on his appearance or on the height of his stature, because I have rejected him. For the LORD sees not as man sees: man looks on the outward appearance, but the LORD looks on the heart." Then Jesse called Abinadab and made him pass before Samuel. And he said, "Neither has the LORD chosen this one." Then Jesse made Shammah pass by. And he said, "Neither has the LORD chosen this one." And Jesse made seven of his sons pass before Samuel. And Samuel said to Jesse, "The LORD has not chosen these." Then Samuel said to Jesse, "Are all your sons here?" And he said, "There remains yet the youngest, but behold, he is keeping the sheep." And Samuel said to Jesse, "Send and get him, for we will not sit down till he comes here." And he sent and brought him in. Now he was ruddy and had beautiful eyes and was handsome. And the LORD said, "Arise, anoint him, for this is he." Then Samuel took the horn of oil and anointed him in the midst of his brothers. And the Spirit of the LORD rushed upon David from that day forward. And Samuel rose up and went to Ramah.

Reflect:

God chose the youngest, the smallest, the one perhaps considered unimportant by his family. God told Samuel not to be swayed by appearances, by human strength, or by the ability to impress. The Lord knows that what matters is a person's heart.

We know from the rest of Scripture that David loved God, trusted God, and knew his need for God. He was a man after God's own heart (Acts 13:22). Samuel was still looking for a king similar to Saul, someone impressive and mighty. But God knew David's desire to please him, to follow hard after him—and this is what truly mattered.

Is there an area in your life where you are tempted to judge by outward appearances, as Samuel did in this passage? God still works through the humble, the lowly, those who know how very much they need him.

As you begin your time of prayer, repent of any ways you are walking in self-sufficiency. Ask for a heart of faith that judges rightly and esteems the same qualities that God esteems. Thank him for his Spirit that is always at work changing our hearts and renewing our souls so that we might know more and more of our need for God.

Pray:

Lord, thank you that you create new hearts within us. Give us the grace to be humble and to love what you love. In Christ's holy name. Amen.

Epiphany Day 10

KARI WEST

Read: *Psalm 65:1–8, 11–13*

Praise is due to you, O God, in Zion,
    and to you shall vows be performed.
O you who hear prayer,
    to you shall all flesh come.
When iniquities prevail against me,
    you atone for our transgressions.
Blessed is the one you choose and bring near,
    to dwell in your courts!
We shall be satisfied with the goodness of your house,
    the holiness of your temple!
By awesome deeds you answer us with righteousness,
    O God of our salvation,
the hope of all the ends of the earth
    and of the farthest seas;
the one who by his strength established the mountains,
    being girded with might;
who stills the roaring of the seas,
    the roaring of their waves,
    the tumult of the peoples,
so that those who dwell at the ends of the earth are in awe at
    your signs.
You make the going out of the morning and the evening to shout
    for joy....
You crown the year with your bounty;
    your wagon tracks overflow with abundance.
The pastures of the wilderness overflow,
    the hills gird themselves with joy,
the meadows clothe themselves with flocks,
    the valleys deck themselves with grain,
    they shout and sing together for joy.

Reflect:

Blessed are those whom God has chosen to bring near to him. Do you often think of your Christian identity in those terms—that you are one chosen to dwell near God? Even more than that now, on this side of the cross, you are the one God chooses to dwell *within*. That is an immeasurable glory and a deep mystery.

He has brought you near, you who were once so far off. He has brought you near—and what a God to be near! What a God who dwells within you! He answers his people with mighty, righteous acts. He stills the roar of the sea and the tumult of the nations. He draws forth songs of joy from the dawn and the setting of the sun. He enriches the soil, directs the rivers, and dresses his world in abundance and gladness.

Creation shouts to its Creator. And we are the ones chosen to be near our Creator God. We are the ones chosen to be indwelt by this abundant, rich, magnificent God.

As you pray, join your voice to the hidden melody of the world and praise God for who he is, what he has done, and how near he is to you.

Pray:

Blessed are those you choose and bring near to live in your courts!
We are filled with the good things of your house, of your holy temple.
You answer us with awesome and righteous deeds, God our Savior, the hope of all the ends of the earth and of the farthest seas. Amen.

(Psalm 65:4–5 NIV)

Epiphany Day 11
WILLA KANE

Read: *Psalm 3*

> O Lord, how many are my foes!
>   Many are rising against me;
> many are saying of my soul,
>   "There is no salvation for him in God." *Selah*
> But you, O Lord, are a shield about me,
>   my glory, and the lifter of my head.
> I cried aloud to the Lord,
>   and he answered me from his holy hill. *Selah*
> I lay down and slept;
>   I woke again, for the Lord sustained me.
> I will not be afraid of many thousands of people
>   who have set themselves against me all around.
> Arise, O Lord!
>   Save me, O my God!
> For you strike all my enemies on the cheek;
>   you break the teeth of the wicked.
> Salvation belongs to the Lord;
>   your blessing be on your people! *Selah*

Reflect:

In Psalm 3, David exposed us to the sadness in his heart as he fled from his own son Absalom, who was trying to kill him and usurp his throne. Many who once followed David were now against him.

Which foes are you facing today? Name them. Cry out to the Lord with your fear, your sadness, and your need.

In David's day, Satan used the lie that God would not save his people. It's the lie Satan still whispers today in a worldly chorus that sows seeds of doubt and discouragement in our hearts. Like David, we have a choice: we can believe the lie of Satan or we can believe our God will save us.

David was sure that God, his shield, would protect him. God, the lifter of his head, would change his perspective. We can be confident of these things too. With God's help, because he lifts our heads, we can look up instead of down. We can fix our eyes on Jesus and not on our circumstances.

As we gaze on our Lord and remember what he died to accomplish, a miraculous thing happens. We see his glory in the gospel, and we are changed. If he has saved us for eternity, how will he not also save us from the daily challenges we face?

Like David, we can go from despondency to trusting in a sure and certain destiny: our names are written with the blood of Christ in the Book of Life. We can lie down and sleep without fear because our God never slumbers or sleeps.

As you pray, lay your heaviness at his feet. Then praise him as the one who hears, answers, delivers, and blesses his people.

Pray:

O soul, are you weary and troubled?
No light in the darkness you see?
There's light for a look at the Savior,
And life more abundant and free.
Turn your eyes upon Jesus,
Look full in His wonderful face,
And the things of earth will grow strangely dim,
In the light of His glory and grace.
Amen.

("Turn Your Eyes upon Jesus" by Helen Howarth Lemmel)

Epiphany Day 12

MADISON PERRY

Read: *Psalm 4*

> Answer me when I call, O God of my righteousness!
>> You have given me relief when I was in distress.
>> Be gracious to me and hear my prayer!
> O men, how long shall my honor be turned into shame?
>> How long will you love vain words and seek after lies? *Selah*
> But know that the LORD has set apart the godly for himself;
>> the LORD hears when I call to him.
> Be angry, and do not sin;
>> ponder in your own hearts on your beds, and be silent. *Selah*
> Offer right sacrifices,
>> and put your trust in the LORD.
> There are many who say, "Who will show us some good?
>> Lift up the light of your face upon us, O LORD!"
> You have put more joy in my heart
>> than they have when their grain and wine abound.
> In peace I will both lie down and sleep;
>> for you alone, O LORD, make me dwell in safety.

Reflect:

In Psalm 4, we find words to live into. As we pray them and let them do their work, we can enjoy fellowship with our God.

When praying these words, we assume the posture of someone who is in need. "Answer me when I call, O God of my righteousness!" (v. 1). This is someone who has had prayers answered before, yet again they find themselves in need of God's provision.

We all know that cycle, and we mustn't feel worn out by it. In this prayer, God gives us words to persevere. He gives us the strength to continue to come to him, and he gives us his love to move us to seek after the good of others. In this life prior to the second coming of our King, problems are never resolved with finality, and tomorrow we will again seek our daily bread.

But we worship the God revealed in Christ, and even when embattled and weak, we have something precious: "You have put more joy in my heart than they have when their grain and wine abound" (v. 7). Even in our fearful days where tomorrow is always up for grabs, we can know the deepest of joys.

This isn't a drunken, over-the-top ecstasy. It is a rooted and peaceful appreciation of God's goodness, known in the ordinary meals, prayers, and passing of time with loved ones. This is the joy of a humble heart, a heart broken and restored by Jesus's life-changing death and resurrection.

Pray that you will trust more deeply that God alone can give you a stable and peaceful joy. As you hear news about our world that makes you anxious, pray that you will turn to Jesus. Pray for strength not to be kidnapped by your fears. Do you know someone who is filled with anxiety? Pray for that person, asking that God will settle his peace and goodness over his or her soul.

Pray:

O God, without whose beauty and goodness our souls are unfed, without whose truth our reason withers: Consecrate our lives to your will, giving us such a purity of heart, such depth of faith, and such steadfastness of purpose, that in time we may come to think your own thoughts after you; through Jesus Christ our Savior. Amen.

(Anglican Church in North America Book of Common Prayer)

Epiphany Day 13
KARI WEST

Read: *Psalm 68:19–20, 24–26, 31–35*

> Blessed be the Lord,
>> who daily bears us up;
>> God is our salvation. *Selah*
> Our God is a God of salvation,
>> and to GOD, the Lord, belong deliverances from death....
> Your procession is seen, O God,
>> the procession of my God, my King, into the sanctuary—
> the singers in front, the musicians last,
>> between them virgins playing tambourines:
> "Bless God in the great congregation,
>> the LORD, O you who are of Israel's fountain!"...
> Nobles shall come from Egypt;
>> Cush shall hasten to stretch out her hands to God.
> O kingdoms of the earth, sing to God;
>> sing praises to the Lord, *Selah*
> to him who rides in the heavens, the ancient heavens;
>> behold, he sends out his voice, his mighty voice.
> Ascribe power to God,
>> whose majesty is over Israel,
>> and whose power is in the skies.
> Awesome is God from his sanctuary;
>> the God of Israel—
>> he is the one who gives power and strength to his people.
> Blessed be God!

Reflect:

God is the one who daily bears us up. God possesses unseen, unending storehouses of power and strength. He promises to act on behalf of his chosen people. In this passage of Scripture, he acts to bring about justice, salvation, and deliverance from death.

Too often we forget our God who rides in the ancient heavens, whose power is in the skies, who reigns in his sanctuary, and who delights in giving strength to his people.

The psalmist imagined a dancing procession of Israelites from the tribes at the farthest edges of the land coming together to praise the Lord in his sanctuary. And then even more broadly, the psalmist said the nations of Cush and Egypt would reach out to the Lord, and the kingdoms of the earth would sing to him.

Are you feeling weak and exhausted today? Are there trials and burdens threatening to overwhelm you? Remember, God daily bears you up. Call to mind this great throng of jubilation rejoicing in the just and salvific acts of our God. Hope in the coming global recognition of his great power, holiness, and deep abiding love. With the psalmist, cry out, "Blessed be God!"

Pray:

Most holy God, the source of all good desires, all right judgements, and all just works: Give to us, your servants, that peace which the world cannot give, so that our minds may be fixed on the doing of your will, and that we, being delivered from the fear of all enemies, may live in peace and quietness; through the mercies of Christ Jesus our Savior. Amen.

(Book of Common Prayer, 1928)

Epiphany Day 14
SALLY BREEDLOVE

Read: *Deuteronomy 33:26–27*

> "There is none like God, O Jeshurun,
>   who rides through the heavens to your help,
>   through the skies in his majesty.
> The eternal God is your dwelling place,
>   and underneath are the everlasting arms."

Reflect:

As Moses faced his own imminent death, his passion was to prepare God's people for a future without his leadership. He urged them to understand that obedience brings blessing and that brokenness and sorrow would follow the choice to turn from God. He reminded them that their time of wandering in the wilderness represented a living picture of the loyal goodness of God and their own stubborn, untrusting hearts.

These verses from Deuteronomy 33 conclude Moses's passionate pleading for the people to trust God. So, how did he sum it all up?

God is your home, Moses told them. *You have lived forty years in the wilderness, but the deeper truth is that you have always been at home in God. He is your safety. No matter what it looks like, you will not fall into the abyss.*

We, too, can bank our lives on Moses's promise. If our trust is in the Lord Jesus Christ, then we are at home. We belong to someone who loves us and keeps us.

Moses's words foreshadow the promise Jesus later makes to all who put their faith in him: "My sheep hear my voice, and I know them, and they follow me. I give them eternal life, and they will never perish, and no one will snatch them out of my hand. My Father, who has given them to me, is greater than all, and no one is able to snatch them out of the Father's hand" (John 10:27–29).

Pray that you will trust and follow the Lord Jesus Christ and that you will know him as your home.

Pray:

We praise you, Lord. Let all our acts of service be acts of prayer done in your name and make all our prayers in your name to be acts of service for this world. Come, Lord Jesus, and bring your kingdom, your peace, and your everlasting life. Amen.

Epiphany Day 15
SALLY BREEDLOVE

Read: *Hebrews 2:10–11, 14–18*

> For it was fitting that he, for whom and by whom all things exist, in bringing many sons to glory, should make the founder of their salvation perfect through suffering. For he who sanctifies and those who are sanctified all have one source....
>
> Since therefore the children share in flesh and blood, he himself likewise partook of the same things, that through death he might destroy the one who has the power of death, that is, the devil, and deliver all those who through fear of death were subject to lifelong slavery. For surely it is not angels that he helps, but he helps the offspring of Abraham. Therefore he had to be made like his brothers in every respect, so that he might become a merciful and faithful high priest in the service of God, to make propitiation for the sins of the people. For because he himself has suffered when tempted, he is able to help those who are being tempted.

Reflect:

The writer of Hebrews assumed we fear death and the loss that death entails. This fear turns us into slaves. We are shackled, the writer of Hebrews said, by our strategies to avoid the inevitable and our attempts to pretend that death in any of its forms will never come to us.

Our fears echo those that accompanied Adam and Eve as God exiled them from the garden. They lost the fullness of God's presence, their deep communion with each other, and their life-giving connection with creation. They lost a true sense of themselves. In some sense, death was magnified. Their lives knew the tentacles of death. That fear has been passed from generation to generation as if it were inscribed in our DNA. We are indeed afraid of death, and that fear makes us slaves.

If someone were to ask you to name your fears or losses, could you make a list? Pause and consider these questions right now: What are you afraid of? How has your fear of death made you a slave?

Christ's death destroyed death's power. We do not need to be afraid of loss. All will be made whole in the age to come. Even now while we still struggle with our fears, with our circumstances, and with the fact that we struggle, Christ's heart toward us is sympathetic, merciful, and faithful. He understands. He wants to help us. He is not ashamed to call us his brothers and sisters.

As you pray, thank Christ that you are not alone, that He understands, and that he wants to help you. Ask him to reveal your fears and to speak his peace to those fears.

Pray:

Most loving Father, please strengthen us to give thanks for all things, to fear nothing but the loss of you, and to cast all our care on the One who cares for us. Preserve us from faithless fears and worldly anxieties, and grant that no clouds of this mortal life may hide us from the light of the love that is immortal and that you have manifested unto us in your Son, Jesus Christ our Lord. Amen.

(adapted from *Anglican Church in North America Book of Common Prayer*)

Epiphany Day 16
SALLY BREEDLOVE

Read: *Job 19:23–27*

> "Oh that my words were written!
>   Oh that they were inscribed in a book!
> Oh that with an iron pen and lead
>   they were engraved in the rock forever!
> For I know that my Redeemer lives,
>   and at the last he will stand upon the earth.
> And after my skin has been thus destroyed,
>   yet in my flesh I shall see God,
> whom I shall see for myself,
>   and my eyes shall behold, and not another.
> My heart faints within me!"

Reflect:

Job's story might confuse you. His friends spoke eloquently about seeking God, doing the right thing, and knowing God's blessing. And Job? He spoke like an angry man, insisting that he must be heard, like a man who had no regard for the advice of his friends.

At the end of the book, God declared that Job's friends did not speak as accurately about God as his servant Job had. And in an act of mercy, God directed Job to offer sacrifices for them and to pray for them.

But exactly how did Job speak rightly about God? He was emotional, confused, and dismissive of his friends' desire to help. Job despaired. He insisted on being heard. He shouted at the heavens. But he never turned his back on God. Everything he said assumed that God really exists, that he listens, and that he hears.

What is the outcome of Job's raw and honest heart? What happens when a person keeps talking to God—rather than about him—in the midst of great pain? In Job's torrent of words, he came to moments of startling insight, as seen in the words of this passage. Job's Redeemer lives. His life would not be over when he died. One day, in his flesh, he would see his Redeemer taking his stand on this earth.

Is this your hope as well? The only sure things are the crucifixion and resurrection of Jesus Christ and the promise that after we die, we will be raised with him.

If you are in a similar season of wrestling and anger, let Job be your teacher. Keep talking to God. Don't turn away from him in cynicism or indifference. Let him see your anger, your confusion, and your despair. When you have said all you need to say, simply be silent and listen. God has not left you. Know that his presence is greater than whatever churns within you. Let God speak or not speak. Simply know he holds you.

Pray:

Lord, you know everything about us and about me. Thank you that you never leave us. Thank you that this life is not the final word. Thank you that one day, in a made-new heaven and earth, you will gather to you all those who are redeemed by the blood of Jesus Christ. Thank you that one day in my new body I will see you face-to-face. In the name of Jesus. Amen.

Epiphany Day 17
SALLY BREEDLOVE

Read: *1 Kings 19:1–8*

Ahab told Jezebel all that Elijah had done, and how he had killed all the prophets with the sword. Then Jezebel sent a messenger to Elijah, saying, "So may the gods do to me and more also, if I do not make your life as the life of one of them by this time tomorrow." Then he was afraid, and he arose and ran for his life and came to Beersheba, which belongs to Judah, and left his servant there.

But he himself went a day's journey into the wilderness and came and sat down under a broom tree. And he asked that he might die, saying, "It is enough; now, O LORD, take away my life, for I am no better than my fathers." And he lay down and slept under a broom tree. And behold, an angel touched him and said to him, "Arise and eat." And he looked, and behold, there was at his head a cake baked on hot stones and a jar of water. And he ate and drank and lay down again. And the angel of the LORD came again a second time and touched him and said, "Arise and eat, for the journey is too great for you." And he arose and ate and drank, and went in the strength of that food forty days and forty nights to Horeb, the mount of God.

Reflect:

Elijah's work had been intense and strongly opposed. He felt that even his friends had turned on him. He was afraid of those in power, so he ran.

God in his mercy does not desert us when we are running away, when we are exhausted, when we have lost hope. That message is part of the big story of the Bible. We see it over and over, from Cain, to Hagar, to Jacob, to Jonah, to Peter, to Paul, and to us. God is the same. He pursues us and he comes to us in Christ Jesus.

Elijah's story in 1 Kings 19 is a picture of God meeting us when we can't go any farther. The angel offered Elijah sleep and food.

It is the same for us. Always God invites us to rest, to trust his provision, even to lie down and sleep in the midst of uncertainty.

As you prepare to pray, consider the angel's words: "The journey is too much for you" (v. 7 NIV). Indeed, it is. We need God's provision: the bread of his Word, the water of his Spirit, the rest that is offered in Jesus Christ. Thank God that you are not in charge of directing, producing, or protecting your own life.

Pray:

Be present, O merciful God, and protect us through the hours of this night, so that we who are wearied by the changes and chances of this life may rest in your eternal changelessness; through Jesus Christ our Lord. Amen.

(Anglican Church in North America Book of Common Prayer)

Epiphany Day 18
WILLA KANE

Read: *Psalm 48:1–3, 9–14*

> Great is the LORD and greatly to be praised
>   in the city of our God!
> His holy mountain, beautiful in elevation,
>   is the joy of all the earth,
> Mount Zion, in the far north,
>   the city of the great King.
> Within her citadels God
>   has made himself known as a fortress....
> We have thought on your steadfast love, O God,
>   in the midst of your temple.
> As your name, O God,
>   so your praise reaches to the ends of the earth.
> Your right hand is filled with righteousness.
>   Let Mount Zion be glad!
> Let the daughters of Judah rejoice
>   because of your judgments!
> Walk about Zion, go around her,
>   number her towers,
> consider well her ramparts,
>   go through her citadels,
> that you may tell the next generation
>   that this is God,
> our God forever and ever.
>   He will guide us forever.

Reflect:

The psalmist began by acknowledging the greatness of the Lord. Because he is great, our response is to praise him for the city that is his own. Jerusalem was a majestic city when this psalm was written. God himself dwelt there in a temple protected by towers, ramparts, and citadels.

Now God dwells through his Spirit in the hearts of his people, as Paul reminded us when he wrote, "Do you not know that you are God's temple and that God's Spirit dwells in you?" (1 Corinthians 3:16). We are his temple, and he is our fortress. Man-made defenses aren't what save God's people. God himself is our Savior and Defender. His steadfast love and his righteousness are our sure defense, our strength, and our glory.

Think about God's steadfast love for you. What has God done for you over the course of your life? Recall the ways he has protected you, led you, and strengthened you. What is God seeking to teach you about his beauty and strength, his power to protect, and his love for you?

Listen to the psalmist's hope: "For this God is our God for ever and ever; he will be our guide even to the end" (Psalm 48:14 NIV). We can be so caught up in our daily routine and in the urgent questions or difficulties we face that we can forget the bigger picture. Whatever testifies to God's love and work is what will stand the test of time. What is it you want to say? What will you be ready to declare about your Father God?

As you pray, remember how far God has brought you. You were once lost, but now you have been found. Thank God for his trustworthy love.

Thank God for the ways he has cared for you, even in the darkness that now faces you. Ask him for ongoing help for yourself and for others. Rejoice, knowing that his victory has already been accomplished in the resurrection of Jesus.

Pray:

Increase, O God, the spirit of neighborliness among us, that in peril we will uphold one another, in suffering tend to one another, and in homelessness, loneliness, or exile befriend one another. Grant us brave and enduring hearts that we may strengthen one another, until the disciplines and testing of these days are ended, and you again give peace in our time; through Jesus Christ our Lord. Amen.

(Anglican Church in North America Book of Common Prayer)

Epiphany Day 19
WILLA KANE

Read: *Romans 15:13*

> May the God of hope fill you with all joy and peace in believing, so
> that by the power of the Holy Spirit you may abound in hope.

Reflect:

Here in Romans 15, the apostle Paul prayed that the lives of Christians would
be characterized by hope, trust (believing), joy, and peace.

Hope is not wishful thinking or finger crossing for some uncertain
outcome. Biblical hope is a confident expectation of good things to come,
rooted in the character of God. We hope in a God whose promises are
certain: "I am God, and there is no other . . . My purpose will stand" (Isaiah
46: 9–10 NIV). We hope in a God who never changes while ruling over
an ever-changing world; he is "the same yesterday and today and forever"
(Hebrews 13:8). We hope in a God whose faithfulness is steadfast: "Let us
hold fast the confession of our hope without wavering, for he who promised
is faithful" (Hebrews 10:23).

Confident hope and trust go together. Trust comes from walking hand
in hand with the God in whom we have placed our hope. Pause to reflect on
where you have been placing your hope of late. Is the Lord Christ your first
and best hope, the one your heart trusts?

With hope and trust as the anchor of our souls, joy and peace are God's
gifts to us to receive and to cultivate in our lives by the power of the Spirit.
Joy is an abiding delight in God that springs from a living, vital relationship
with him through our Lord Jesus Christ. Peace comes from knowing whose
you are and where your life will ultimately lead. Creation in its present state
and everything in it is passing away. Our future hope is in the dawning of a
new creation and in eternal life with Christ.

Recentering ourselves on these truths can transform the way that we
live out our day-to-day lives. As you come to pray, renew your trust in the

God of hope, receive the joy and peace of life in Christ, and ask that God will empower you to exemplify these fruits of the Spirit to those around you.

Pray:

Lord Jesus, stay with us, for evening is at hand and the day is past; be our companion in the way, kindle our hearts, and awaken hope, that we may know thee as thou art revealed in Scripture and the breaking of bread. Grant this for the sake of thy love. Amen.

(Anglican Church in North America Book of Common Prayer)

Epiphany Day 20
SALLY BREEDLOVE

Read: *Deuteronomy 8:3–16*

And he humbled you and let you hunger and fed you with manna, which you did not know, nor did your fathers know, that he might make you know that man does not live by bread alone, but man lives by every word that comes from the mouth of the LORD. Your clothing did not wear out on you and your foot did not swell these forty years. Know then in your heart that, as a man disciplines his son, the LORD your God disciplines you. So you shall keep the commandments of the LORD your God by walking in his ways and by fearing him. For the LORD your God is bringing you into a good land, a land of brooks of water, of fountains and springs, flowing out in the valleys and hills, a land of wheat and barley, of vines and fig trees and pomegranates, a land of olive trees and honey, a land in which you will eat bread without scarcity, in which you will lack nothing, a land whose stones are iron, and out of whose hills you can dig copper. And you shall eat and be full, and you shall bless the LORD your God for the good land he has given you.

Take care lest you forget the LORD your God by not keeping his commandments and his rules and his statutes, which I command you today, lest, when you have eaten and are full and have built good houses and live in them, and when your herds and flocks multiply and your silver and gold is multiplied and all that you have is multiplied, then your heart be lifted up, and you forget the LORD your God, who brought you out of the land of Egypt, out of the house of slavery, who led you through the great and terrifying wilderness, with its fiery serpents and scorpions and thirsty ground where there was no water, who brought you water out of the flinty rock, who fed you in the wilderness with manna that your fathers did not know, that he might humble you and test you, to do you good in the end.

Reflect:

Moses's audience in Deuteronomy was primarily the young people of Israel. What would you want the next generation to know? Would you want them to know how badly their parents had gone off course or the dire consequences of choosing disobedience? Perhaps you'd paint a compelling picture of the good and prosperous future that God has planned for them.

Moses would preach those things in Deuteronomy, but here his focus was the faithful, fatherly love of God. Yes, God had trained them by trial, but his people were not boot camp recruits under the heavy hand of a harsh sergeant. They were not world-class spiritual athletes being trained by a coach who always demanded more, more, more.

Moses knew what God is like, so he reminded the people that God himself is Father and that God's plan has always been to do his people good. When Satan tempted Jesus in the wilderness, Jesus recalled this passage. Jesus trusted his Father's care and his Father's provision. Knowing the end is good grows hope and endurance in us as well.

As you begin your time of prayer, contemplate a season of past trial in your own life. What would you tell others about that time? Do you see it as a wilderness, or do you have a different story? Are there ways the trials you have endured have helped you see more clearly how your heart is broken and misshapen? How have you seen the goodness of God in those barren and terrifying places? And most of all, have you come to know by experience that God is indeed Immanuel? He is God with us, and in the end, he always does us good.

Pray:

O God, grant that we may desire you, and desiring you seek you, and seeking you find you, and finding you be satisfied in you for ever. Amen

(Francis Xavier)

Epiphany Day 21
MADISON PERRY

Read: *Psalm 5:1–11*

> Give ear to my words, O LORD;
>> consider my groaning.
> Give attention to the sound of my cry,
>> my King and my God,
>> for to you do I pray.
> O LORD, in the morning you hear my voice;
>> in the morning I prepare a sacrifice for you and watch.
> For you are not a God who delights in wickedness;
>> evil may not dwell with you.
> The boastful shall not stand before your eyes;
>> you hate all evildoers.
> You destroy those who speak lies;
>> the LORD abhors the bloodthirsty and deceitful man.
> But I, through the abundance of your steadfast love,
>> will enter your house.
> I will bow down toward your holy temple
>> in the fear of you.
> Lead me, O LORD, in your righteousness
>> because of my enemies;
>> make your way straight before me.
> For there is no truth in their mouth;
>> their inmost self is destruction;
> their throat is an open grave;
>> they flatter with their tongue.
> Make them bear their guilt, O God;
>> let them fall by their own counsels;
> because of the abundance of their transgressions cast them out,
>> for they have rebelled against you.
> But let all who take refuge in you rejoice;
>> let them ever sing for joy,
> and spread your protection over them,
>> that those who love your name may exult in you.

Reflect:

In this psalm, King David led us into the throne room of God, the center of heaven and earth. This is not a moment of cozy comfort but one of respect and splendor that will lead us to immense joy. For even in so grand a place as God's throne room, David told God, "I, through the abundance of your steadfast love, will enter your house" (v. 7). None of us deserves to be here, but we are welcomed by a great love.

David asked for the righteousness of God, a gift that we know comes through Jesus Christ, who humbled himself under death so that we could be lifted up. Remember how undeserving you feel to be in the throne room of the Most High God. When we are covered in God's righteousness, we are transformed into sons and daughters of this King. Then, we will be moved as David was to encourage others to sing for joy. This is the consequence of that radical love that welcomes us in—it lifts us up, fills us, and gives us peace.

This psalm is not a thought experiment. It is real—more real than any other news or opportunities you have heard of today. If you will submit to God and ask him for the righteousness of Christ, then he will surely give it.

Be led into God's throne room by the blood of Christ. Take refuge here and claim it in faith as a resting place of joy. Pray for someone you know who does not know God as his or her refuge. Pray that this person will know that God stands ready to hear his or her cry. Look for a moment at your own heart: where do you turn when you hear more bad news? Ask God to give you a heart that runs to him first.

Pray:

Hear my cry, O God, listen to my prayer; from the end of the earth I call to you when my heart is faint. Lead me to the rock that is higher than I, for you have been my refuge, a strong tower against the enemy. Let me dwell in your tent forever! Let me take refuge under the shelter of your wings! Amen.

(Psalm 61:1–4)

Epiphany Day 22

MADISON PERRY

Read: *Psalm 6*

> O LORD, rebuke me not in your anger,
>> nor discipline me in your wrath.
> Be gracious to me, O LORD, for I am languishing;
>> heal me, O LORD, for my bones are troubled.
> My soul also is greatly troubled.
>> But you, O LORD—how long?
> Turn, O LORD, deliver my life;
>> save me for the sake of your steadfast love.
> For in death there is no remembrance of you;
>> in Sheol who will give you praise?
> I am weary with my moaning;
>> every night I flood my bed with tears;
>> I drench my couch with my weeping.
> My eye wastes away because of grief;
>> it grows weak because of all my foes.
> Depart from me, all you workers of evil,
>> for the LORD has heard the sound of my weeping.
> The LORD has heard my plea;
>> the LORD accepts my prayer.
> All my enemies shall be ashamed and greatly troubled;
>> they shall turn back and be put to shame in a moment.

Reflect:

No matter where we turn, no matter what we have achieved, no matter what we have earned, lost, or forfeited, the riches of the grace of God are on offer right now. The riches of the world are dust compared to this, the glory of knowing God.

That is why David turned to the Lord every day. His surrounding circumstances were often different, but his goal was the same. He came seeking life.

While external worries often drive us to the Lord, there is an internal struggle that threatens our relationship with God. And it is this inner battle that we witness as David faced God's wrath at the start of this psalm. "Be gracious to me, O LORD, for I am languishing; heal me, O LORD, for my bones are troubled" (v. 2).

We, like David, have welcomed sin into our lives through countless doors. It lives with us now, often out of sight. Come to the Lord and ask him to save you in his steadfast love. Honestly reckon with the powerful vices you carry in reserve.

Our Father wants to make your heart a deep well filled with the Spirit of his Son, a fountain from which love flows to a hurting world. Come and ask him to renovate your heart. For those of us who have approached Jesus before and asked him to take our sin, there remain new depths to which Christ's grace will penetrate if only we will ask. Ask him to forgive you, to cleanse you, and to bring you into a right relationship with him.

As you pray, take a moment to call to mind the great mercy of God. He knows all about you and yet still calls you his beloved son or daughter in Jesus. We have not been abandoned. Thank him for his mercy and forgiveness. Think of someone you love who is burdened by failures and closed in by shame. Pray that this person comes to know how dearly his or her Father in heaven loves him or her.

Pray:

Lord, you say that if we confess our sins, you are faithful and just to forgive us our sin and to cleanse us from all unrighteousness. Because of your grace and mercy, I confess to you the things I have done wrong this day, the good things I have left undone, and the sinful thoughts and intentions of my heart. Trusting in your great mercy, here is my confession: [Here, mention those things you need to confess]. Amen.

Epiphany Day 23
MADISON PERRY

Read: *Psalm 8*

> O LORD, our Lord,
>> how majestic is your name in all the earth!
>
> You have set your glory above the heavens.
>> Out of the mouth of babies and infants,
>
> you have established strength because of your foes,
>> to still the enemy and the avenger.
>
> When I look at your heavens, the work of your fingers,
>> the moon and the stars, which you have set in place,
>
> what is man that you are mindful of him,
>> and the son of man that you care for him?
>
> Yet you have made him a little lower than the heavenly beings
>> and crowned him with glory and honor.
>
> You have given him dominion over the works of your hands;
>> you have put all things under his feet,
>
> all sheep and oxen,
>> and also the beasts of the field,
>
> the birds of the heavens, and the fish of the sea,
>> whatever passes along the paths of the seas.
>
> O LORD, our Lord,
>> how majestic is your name in all the earth!

Reflect:

This psalm is an invitation to step into a new world, a world where every square inch of creation testifies to our Creator.

Whether you know it or not, this world is made to be a vessel for God's glory, an intricately arranged diorama where each element is meant to reflect the stunning light that shines from the face of Christ. Stars reflect the glory of God, as do fish, sheep, oxen, and birds. Have you passed through the day without realizing that this world is a marvel? This psalm challenges us to pause and thank the Lord for the gifts we have been given, from the air we breathe to the trees we have barely noticed. This is part of our role as priestly stewards of creation—to encounter God's glory in creation and turn that encounter into prayer.

No bird is just a bird. All creation is meant to be a vessel for God's glory. And amid all this intricacy and great intention, we come to God's magnificent achievement in people.

This too can be surprising. We see each other midstream, in the middle of our movement from birth to natural death. It is easy to forget that the people who pester you, baffle you, and otherwise offend your sensibilities are made "a little lower than the angels" and are crowned with "glory and honor" (v. 5 NIV). God desires that all his children should be saved and become humble bearers of his glory.

Pause now and recall the majesty of God revealed in the created order. Consider the places you have been called to steward this world, to care for plants, animals, land, and people. Thank the Lord for the whole range of people in your life—friends, family, neighbors, enemies. Pray that the Lord will be at work to bring them humility and wisdom as well as the ability to join you in praise of our God.

Pray:

O Lord, our Lord, how majestic is your name in all the earth! We praise you for our creation, our preservation, and all the blessings of this life. We ask that all people might be brought within the reach of your saving embrace, that they might serve you in thought, word, and deed and know your eternal life. May your Holy Spirit be at work, drawing more and more people unto you. Amen.

Epiphany Day 24
MADISON PERRY

Read: *Psalm 13*

> How long, O Lord? Will you forget me forever?
>> How long will you hide your face from me?
> How long must I take counsel in my soul
>> and have sorrow in my heart all the day?
> How long shall my enemy be exalted over me?
> Consider and answer me, O Lord my God;
>> light up my eyes, lest I sleep the sleep of death,
> lest my enemy say, "I have prevailed over him,"
>> lest my foes rejoice because I am shaken.
> But I have trusted in your steadfast love;
>> my heart shall rejoice in your salvation.
> I will sing to the Lord,
>> because he has dealt bountifully with me.

Reflect:

Are you in a long season of waiting on the Lord?

In this psalm, David reported having "sorrow in [his] heart all the day" (v. 2). He turned to the Lord, and finding little counsel, he had only his own soul for that purpose. He was isolated and felt the approach of death.

But in verses 5 and 6, there is a turning point:

> But I have trusted in your steadfast love;
> my heart shall rejoice in your salvation.
> I will sing to the Lord,
> because he has dealt bountifully with me.

Here, in the face of his present sense of abandonment, David remembered the Lord's salvation, an event so great that even the present circumstances couldn't threaten it. David had been saved, and he remembered it. As he turned to God in praise, he understood his life very differently. The Father's love had never left him, but now he remembered it—and now he would trust it and would sing to him. This is an eternal love that outlasted every circumstance David faced; this love will also outlast every crisis that assails us.

As you pray, ask God how long you will have to wait. Let the question hang. Ask how long your suffering or difficulty will continue. Be honest. Now recall your salvation and trust in God. Remember God's love, your betrayal of him in sin, and the salvation and promise of Jesus Christ. Rejoice in that salvation that shines bright even now, in the midst of hardship.

Pray:

Father, in the midst of great troubles, we rest in your arms. You have given us the greatest salvation and have caused us to be reborn to a living hope through the resurrection of Jesus Christ. We praise you for your victory over death! May the whole world come to know this salvation and restoration. Help us to continue trusting you. Please, Lord, let your kingdom come in all its fullness, and be at work in the present moment. Amen.

Epiphany Day 25
ELIZABETH GATEWOOD

Read: *Isaiah 28:2–4, 14–17*

> Behold, the Lord has one who is mighty and strong;
>> like a storm of hail, a destroying tempest,
> like a storm of mighty, overflowing waters,
>> he casts down to the earth with his hand.
> The proud crown of the drunkards of Ephraim
>> will be trodden underfoot;
> and the fading flower of its glorious beauty,
>> which is on the head of the rich valley,
> will be like a first-ripe fig before the summer:
>> when someone sees it, he swallows it
>> as soon as it is in his hand....
> Therefore hear the word of the LORD, you scoffers,
>> who rule this people in Jerusalem!
> Because you have said, "We have made a covenant with death,
>> and with Sheol we have an agreement,
> when the overwhelming whip passes through
>> it will not come to us,
> for we have made lies our refuge,
>> and in falsehood we have taken shelter";
> therefore thus says the Lord GOD,
> "Behold, I am the one who has laid as a foundation in Zion,
>> a stone, a tested stone,
> a precious cornerstone, of a sure foundation:
>> 'Whoever believes will not be in haste.'
> And I will make justice the line,
>> and righteousness the plumb line;
> and hail will sweep away the refuge of lies,
>> and waters will overwhelm the shelter."

Reflect:

The prophet Isaiah spoke vivid words of woe to the leaders of Israel and Judah. They had settled for cheap beauty. They had settled for pithy morality and spiritual wisdom, distorting God's Words into a list of rules.

They had settled for false assurances and protection by making a covenant with death instead of turning to the living God.

These things we turn to will not last. And still, when we experience their failure, we grieve. God invites us away from these idols and to the cornerstone of Jesus Christ. In him, we see true beauty, not the cheap and fading beauty of an image-obsessed culture. In him, we see the true spiritual wisdom of being united with Christ. In baptism, we have been joined to him in his death and have been raised with Christ. We no longer need false assurances and imagined protections against death, because we are sealed to Christ's life.

God will set his people free. He will build something more enduring than their idols: the cornerstone. He will build something new, marked by righteousness and justice, something where false beauty, false spirituality, and false hope will have no place. He will build a sure foundation that cannot be shaken.

As you pray, consider where you are settling for false beauty, pithy morality, and empty hope. Imagine the downpour of God's severe mercy washing away your idols and turning you toward the cornerstone that is Jesus Christ.

Pray:

God, we grieve when our idols tumble and crumble and our facades of beauty, truth, and control fade. We do not know what else to do. We cannot see in these moments your severe mercy coming to us in the form of cleansing judgment. We cling to our meager substitutions, accustomed to this cheap fare. It feels painful. Yet you offer us nothing less than yourself—true magnificent beauty, righteousness by being joined to your very body and sealed by the Holy Spirit, and everlasting life in Christ. As Isaiah wrote, your plan is wonderful and your wisdom magnificent. Would you bring the rain of your cleansing grace and, in your tenderness, walk with us? Amen.

Epiphany Day 26
WILLA KANE

Read: *Isaiah 29:13–19*

And the Lord said:
"Because this people draw near with their mouth
    and honor me with their lips,
      while their hearts are far from me,
and their fear of me is a commandment taught by men,
therefore, behold, I will again
    do wonderful things with this people,
      with wonder upon wonder;
and the wisdom of their wise men shall perish,
      and the discernment of their discerning men shall be hidden."
Ah, you who hide deep from the LORD your counsel,
      whose deeds are in the dark,
      and who say, "Who sees us? Who knows us?"
You turn things upside down!
Shall the potter be regarded as the clay,
that the thing made should say of its maker,
    "He did not make me";
or the thing formed say of him who formed it,
    "He has no understanding"?
Is it not yet a very little while
    until Lebanon shall be turned into a fruitful field,
    and the fruitful field shall be regarded as a forest?
In that day the deaf shall hear
    the words of a book,
and out of their gloom and darkness
    the eyes of the blind shall see.
The meek shall obtain fresh joy in the LORD,
    and the poor among mankind shall exult in the Holy One of
    Israel.

Reflect:

The prophet Isaiah indicted his contemporaries for something we're guilty of today: having a wayward heart while paying lip service to the one true God. Thankfully, God's indictment doesn't simply end in judgment.

Isaiah said, "Because this people draw near with their mouth and honor me with their lips, while their hearts are far from me, and their fear of me is a commandment taught by men, therefore, behold, I will again do wonderful things with this people" (v. 13).

Because these people say the right things and act out worship even though their hearts aren't in it, God offers this shocking response.

"*Therefore, behold*, I will again do wonderful things with this people, with wonder upon wonder."

What causes him to transform lives, to bring fruit into barrenness, hearing to deaf ears, sight to blind eyes, joy to the meek, and exultation to the poor? Why turn the world on its head, expose the wise as fools, and turn from those who think they have the inside track for prosperity?

The Potter whose hands mold the clay, the Maker who made all things, is a God of grace and mercy. In love, at Christ's expense, he withholds punishment and gives what we don't deserve. This Jesus, wonder of wonder, came as a baby child, the Holy One of Israel, into a world dark and broken. In glory, he will come again to draw us to himself.

As you pray, confess your wandering heart and cold worship, doing religion but not relationship. Bring your brokenness before the one who made all things and be made whole. Rejoice.

Pray:

Grant, Almighty God, that the words we have heard this day with our ears may by your grace be grafted in our hearts, that they may bring forth in us the fruit of a righteous life, to the honor and praise of your Name; through Jesus Christ our Lord. Amen.

(Anglican Church in North America Book of Common Prayer)

Epiphany Day 27
NATHAN BAXTER

Read: *Isaiah 30:8, 15–18*

> And now, go, write it before them on a tablet
> and inscribe it in a book,
> that it may be for the time to come
> as a witness forever....
> For thus said the Lord GOD, the Holy One of Israel,
> "In returning and rest you shall be saved;
> in quietness and in trust shall be your strength."
> But you were unwilling, and you said,
> "No! We will flee upon horses";
> therefore you shall flee away;
> and, "We will ride upon swift steeds";
> therefore your pursuers shall be swift.
> A thousand shall flee at the threat of one;
> at the threat of five you shall flee,
> till you are left
> like a flagstaff on the top of a mountain,
> like a signal on a hill.
> Therefore the LORD waits to be gracious to you,
> and therefore he exalts himself to show mercy to you.
> For the LORD is a God of justice;
> blessed are all those who wait for him.

Reflect:

Isn't it strange how ancient words can transcend time and place to resonate here and now? Yet is this not God's gracious design for these and other Scriptures?

God instructed Isaiah to write down what he spoke then so that ears in later times would hear. Hundreds of years later, another Spirit-moved writer, Paul, declared, "Everything that was written in the past was written to teach us, so that through the endurance taught in the Scriptures and the encouragement they provide we might have hope" (Romans 15:4 NIV).

"The LORD [who] longs to be gracious," who is also "a God of justice" (Isaiah 30:18 NIV), speaks patiently though earnestly across the centuries to any who will turn again to listen, settle in with his Word, and remain quiet long enough to begin trusting.

As you ponder the Scriptures as a way into prayer, take heart from the promised blessing of Isaiah 30:18. Wait with and for God.

Pray:

Our God, in whom we trust: Strengthen us not to regard overmuch who is for us or who is against us, but to see to it that we be with you in everything we do. Amen.

(Thomas à Kempis)

Epiphany Day 28
NATHAN BAXTER

Read: *Isaiah 31:1–7*

Woe to those who go down to Egypt for help
and rely on horses,
who trust in chariots because they are many
and in horsemen because they are very strong,
but do not look to the Holy One of Israel
or consult the LORD!
And yet he is wise and brings disaster;
he does not call back his words,
but will arise against the house of the evildoers
and against the helpers of those who work iniquity.
The Egyptians are man, and not God,
and their horses are flesh, and not spirit.
When the LORD stretches out his hand,
the helper will stumble, and he who is helped will fall,
and they will all perish together.
For thus the LORD said to me,
"As a lion or a young lion growls over his prey,
and when a band of shepherds is called out against him
he is not terrified by their shouting
or daunted at their noise,
so the LORD of hosts will come down
to fight on Mount Zion and on its hill.
Like birds hovering, so the LORD of hosts
will protect Jerusalem;
he will protect and deliver it;
he will spare and rescue it."

Turn to him from whom people have deeply revolted, O children of Israel. For in that day everyone shall cast away his idols of silver and his idols of gold, which your hands have sinfully made for you.

Reflect:

Friends and allies are vital for safety in a world ruled by the sword. What might happen to us if we realized that in this violent world, we could count on Jesus to be our ally and our friend?

Epiphany is an invitation to consider the fullness of what it means to believe that in the baby Jesus, God came among us to dwell in human flesh. And this same Jesus declared himself to be our friend, the friend who will never leave us, and the friend who has overcome the world.

But still it is easy for us, like it was for Israel, to be threatened by the chaos and evil of the world around us. Yes, the baby Jesus is beautiful to consider. But how can he help us now, in our day, with threats all around us?

How easily God's people then and now forget that "he too is wise and . . . does not take back his words" (v. 2 NIV). How easily we forget that one day he will rise up against all evil and conquer it. God's heart is to protect and deliver us, to spare and rescue us. He is doing just that, even now. Christ has triumphed on the cross, he is raised from the dead, and he will come again.

Though we may forget our truest Friend and wisest Ally, God does not forget us. And he calls us away from the unstable security of the sword and every other idol that disappoints.

"Return," God says to his fickle friends. Return, not to be shamed but to be saved.

As you turn to prayer, ask God your Friend to shift your alliances so that you can trust him more deeply.

Pray:

O God of peace, who has taught us that in returning and rest we shall be saved, in quietness and confidence shall be our strength: By the might of your Spirit lift us, we pray, to your presence, where we may be still and know that you are God; through Jesus Christ our Lord. Amen.

(adapted from *Anglican Church in North America Book of Common Prayer*)

Epiphany Day 29
NATHAN BAXTER

Read: *Isaiah 32:1–8*

> Behold, a king will reign in righteousness,
> > and princes will rule in justice.
> Each will be like a hiding place from the wind,
> > a shelter from the storm,
> like streams of water in a dry place,
> > like the shade of a great rock in a weary land.
> Then the eyes of those who see will not be closed,
> > and the ears of those who hear will give attention.
> The heart of the hasty will understand and know,
> > and the tongue of the stammerers will hasten to speak
> > distinctly.
> The fool will no more be called noble,
> > nor the scoundrel said to be honorable.
> For the fool speaks folly,
> > and his heart is busy with iniquity,
> to practice ungodliness,
> > to utter error concerning the LORD,
> to leave the craving of the hungry unsatisfied,
> > and to deprive the thirsty of drink.
> As for the scoundrel—his devices are evil;
> > he plans wicked schemes
> to ruin the poor with lying words,
> > even when the plea of the needy is right.
> But he who is noble plans noble things,
> > and on noble things he stands.

Reflect:

In the stormy times we inhabit (perhaps not so different from other times in history), we rightly long for leaders and rulers like Jesus. We rightly long for a clear-sighted, open-eared society where even the fearful-hearted and hesitant can know and understand.

The Righteous Ruler entered our scoundrel-filled world, set new creation in motion, ascended to the "right hand of the Majesty on high," and waits patiently for his enemies to be confounded (Hebrews 1:3).

We may hear folly and lament the spread of error. Evil schemes may prevail for a time. Lies may overwhelm the poor and needy. Still, the noble ones who take shelter in King Jesus may make noble plans and stand by noble deeds, even in a storm.

As you pray, bring the stormy parts of your life and the world into the shelter of God's presence. Be still with him and listen. Might he be nudging you to collaborate with him in noble plans or deeds?

Pray:

O Rock divine, O Refuge dear,
A Shelter in the time of storm;
Be Thou our Helper ever near,
A Shelter in the time of storm.

("A Shelter in the Time of Storm" by Vernon J. Charlesworth)

Epiphany Day 30
NATHAN BAXTER

Read: *Isaiah 33:1–6*

> Ah, you destroyer,
>> who yourself have not been destroyed,
>
> you traitor,
>> whom none has betrayed!
>
> When you have ceased to destroy,
>> you will be destroyed;
>
> and when you have finished betraying,
>> they will betray you.
>
> O Lord, be gracious to us; we wait for you.
>> Be our arm every morning,
>> our salvation in the time of trouble.
>
> At the tumultuous noise peoples flee;
>> when you lift yourself up, nations are scattered,
>
> and your spoil is gathered as the caterpillar gathers;
>> as locusts leap, it is leapt upon.
>
> The Lord is exalted, for he dwells on high;
>> he will fill Zion with justice and righteousness,
>
> and he will be the stability of your times,
>> abundance of salvation, wisdom, and knowledge;
>> the fear of the Lord is Zion's treasure.

Reflect:

Many value creativity, and yet destructiveness is all too easy, far too common. Many more value loyalty, and yet betrayals are all too common, far too easy.

Perhaps these desires for creativity and loyalty signal our longing for their source: the Creator, whose loyal and generative love is fresh every morning.

As you pray, make Isaiah 33:2 the core of your petition: "Lord, be gracious to us; we long for you. Be our strength every morning, our salvation in time of distress" (NIV).

Make Isaiah 33:5 a springboard for adoration and hope: "The LORD is exalted, for he dwells on high; he will fill Zion with his justice and righteousness" (NIV).

Trust Isaiah 33:6 as the key to true treasure and prevailing prayer: "He will be the sure foundation for your times, a rich store of salvation and wisdom and knowledge; the fear of the LORD is the key to this treasure" (NIV).

Pray:

Most loving Father, you will us to give thanks for all things, to dread nothing but the loss of you, and to cast all our care on the One who cares for us. Preserve us from faithless fears and worldly anxieties, and grant that no clouds of this mortal life may hide from us the light of that love which is immortal, and which you have manifested unto us in your Son, Jesus Christ our Lord. Amen.

(Anglican Church in North America Book of Common Prayer)

Epiphany Day 31
NATHAN BAXTER

Read: *Isaiah 34:8–15*

>For the LORD has a day of vengeance,
>   a year of recompense for the cause of Zion.
>And the streams of Edom shall be turned into pitch,
>   and her soil into sulfur;
>   her land shall become burning pitch.
>Night and day it shall not be quenched;
>   its smoke shall go up forever.
>From generation to generation it shall lie waste;
>   none shall pass through it forever and ever.
>But the hawk and the porcupine shall possess it,
>   the owl and the raven shall dwell in it.
>He shall stretch the line of confusion over it,
>   and the plumb line of emptiness.
>Its nobles—there is no one there to call it a kingdom,
>   and all its princes shall be nothing.
>Thorns shall grow over its strongholds,
>   nettles and thistles in its fortresses.
>It shall be the haunt of jackals,
>   an abode for ostriches.
>And wild animals shall meet with hyenas;
>   the wild goat shall cry to his fellow;
>indeed, there the night bird settles and
>   finds for herself a resting place.
>There the owl nests and lays
>   and hatches and gathers her young in her shadow;
>indeed, there the hawks are gathered,
>   each one with her mate.

Reflect:

The prophetic passages that speak of God's judgment on oppression, violence, and lawlessness make many people uncomfortable. But rightly heard, they can be sources of hope and directions for prayer.

Isaiah 34 speaks of God's decisive and final removal of violence and oppression from the new creation he is preparing to reveal. All of the wars we have ever witnessed or read about have been, at best, temporary and partial remedies for greater wrongs. Oppression, violence, and lawlessness return all too soon.

How seldom we see the predators of nature at rest and nesting or nurturing. How seldom scavengers cease their post-carnage work. More seldom still do the predators and scavengers of human society rest, or change, or meet their ends.

Yet prophetic hope promises a day when all evils will be not slowed but stopped, not curbed but crushed. That hope can be fulfilled only by the God in whom both justice and mercy shine.

As you pray, consider the measuring line of chaos and the plumb line of desolation, and yield your hopes for righteousness and peace to the only one who does all things well.

Pray:

Eternal God, in whose perfect kingdom no sword is drawn but the sword of righteousness, no strength known but the strength of love: So mightily spread abroad your Spirit, that all peoples may be gathered under the banner of the Prince of Peace; to whom be dominion and glory, now and forever. Amen.

(Anglican Church in North America Book of Common Prayer)

Epiphany Day 32
NATHAN BAXTER

Read: *Isaiah 35:5–10*

> Then the eyes of the blind shall be opened,
>> and the ears of the deaf unstopped;
> then shall the lame man leap like a deer,
>> and the tongue of the mute sing for joy.
> For waters break forth in the wilderness,
>> and streams in the desert;
> the burning sand shall become a pool,
>> and the thirsty ground springs of water;
> in the haunt of jackals, where they lie down,
>> the grass shall become reeds and rushes.
> And a highway shall be there,
>> and it shall be called the Way of Holiness;
> the unclean shall not pass over it.
>> It shall belong to those who walk on the way;
>> even if they are fools, they shall not go astray.
> No lion shall be there,
>> nor shall any ravenous beast come up on it;
> they shall not be found there,
>> but the redeemed shall walk there.
> And the ransomed of the LORD shall return
>> and come to Zion with singing;
> everlasting joy shall be upon their heads;
>> they shall obtain gladness and joy,
>> and sorrow and sighing shall flee away.

Reflect:

God's judgment transformed a kingdom into a wasteland and "a haunt of jackals," but that same place ultimately becomes the scene of God's recreation. Where judgment fell, mercy and renewal spring up.

Isaiah wrote of a future prosperity for Israel, an undoing of judgment that is so complete that joy and holiness break in and overcome every devastation.

Jesus revealed that he himself is the way, the truth, and the life. He is that highway of holiness to the Father.

What is the landscape around your life right now? What is the landscape of your soul? Listen to the words we are offered by Isaiah: burning sand, thirsty ground, uncleanness, fools, ravenous beasts.

Or—streams in the desert, a way of holiness that takes us out of the desert, redemption, ransom, everlasting joy.

Who could make a path out of the torment of the desert? Only Jesus. The way out is the way of the cross, where Jesus bore all judgment for the depredations of rebel humankind. The place where Jesus hung parched now flows with living water. The place where the cry of dereliction went up is now the place where sounds of joy rise up. The place where scavengers cast lots for cast-off clothing is now the place where redeemed people find robes of righteousness and garments of praise.

As you move to prayer, rejoice in anticipation of the day when gladness and joy will overtake you in all your desolate places. And as you rise from prayer, join him on that holy highway.

Pray:

O God of unchangeable power and eternal light: Look favorably on your whole Church, that wonderful and sacred mystery; by the effectual working of your providence, carry out in tranquility the plan of salvation; let the whole world see and know that things that were cast down are being raised up, and that things which had grown old are being made new, and that all things are being brought to their perfection by him through whom all things were made, your Son Jesus Christ our Lord. Amen.

(Anglican Church in North America Book of Common Prayer)

Epiphany Day 33
KARI WEST

Read: *Isaiah 38:1–8*

In those days Hezekiah became sick and was at the point of death. And Isaiah the prophet the son of Amoz came to him, and said to him, "Thus says the LORD: Set your house in order, for you shall die, you shall not recover." Then Hezekiah turned his face to the wall and prayed to the LORD, and said, "Please, O LORD, remember how I have walked before you in faithfulness and with a whole heart, and have done what is good in your sight." And Hezekiah wept bitterly.

Then the word of the LORD came to Isaiah: "Go and say to Hezekiah, Thus says the LORD, the God of David your father: I have heard your prayer; I have seen your tears. Behold, I will add fifteen years to your life. I will deliver you and this city out of the hand of the king of Assyria, and will defend this city.

"This shall be the sign to you from the LORD, that the LORD will do this thing that he has promised: Behold, I will make the shadow cast by the declining sun on the dial of Ahaz turn back ten steps." So the sun turned back on the dial the ten steps by which it had declined.

Reflect:

God hears prayer and responds to it. Somehow, in the mystery of his sovereignty and our human freedom, prayer moves the hand of God. In this passage, God saw Hezekiah's tears, listened to his words, and then granted his requests—both personal deliverance from his illness and the city's deliverance from the Assyrian king. Not only that, but God also granted a miraculous sign to assure Hezekiah of his promises. He pulled back the sun's shadow.

Illness was beaten, death was cheated, an evil ruler was routed, and the shadow retreated—leaving the sun to shine in all its brightness.

Such is the power of prayer. God delights to answer his people. Will you come before him and trust that he hears you, that he catches each of your tears, and that he bears your burdens? Father to child, friend to friend, husband to wife—these are the barest echoes of what he is to you.

He will rise with healing in his wings. He will trample death again. He will conquer all evil. He will retract all shadows. We won't need the sun's brightness, for the Lord will be our everlasting light.

Pray:

Lord Jesus, stay with us, for evening is at hand and the day is past; be our companion in the way, kindle our hearts, and awaken hope, that we may know you as you are revealed in Scripture and the breaking of bread. Grant this for the sake of your love. Amen.

(Anglican Church in North America Book of Common Prayer)

Epiphany Day 34
KARI WEST

Read: *Isaiah 40:11, 25–31*

> He will tend his flock like a shepherd;
>> he will gather the lambs in his arms;
> he will carry them in his bosom,
>> and gently lead those that are with young....
> To whom then will you compare me,
>> that I should be like him? says the Holy One.
> Lift up your eyes on high and see:
>> who created these?
> He who brings out their host by number,
>> calling them all by name;
> by the greatness of his might
>> and because he is strong in power,
>> not one is missing.
> Why do you say, O Jacob,
>> and speak, O Israel,
> "My way is hidden from the LORD,
>> and my right is disregarded by my God"?
> Have you not known? Have you not heard?
> The LORD is the everlasting God,
>> the Creator of the ends of the earth.
> He does not faint or grow weary;
>> his understanding is unsearchable.
> He gives power to the faint,
>> and to him who has no might he increases strength.
> Even youths shall faint and be weary,
>> and young men shall fall exhausted;
> but they who wait for the LORD shall renew their strength;
>> they shall mount up with wings like eagles;
> they shall run and not be weary;
>> they shall walk and not faint.

Reflect:

What a beautiful juxtaposition we find in these verses between might and tenderness, vast power and personal love, awe-inspiring majesty and gentle care. God pulls out the starry host; he measures the nations as dust on the scales; he holds the vast oceans in the hollow of his hand; he sits enthroned in the heavens. And God tends to his people gently; he carries them as lambs, close to his heart. He draws near and empowers the weak and the weary.

This is your God. He is tending to you as the perfect Shepherd to his flock—protecting, guiding, and cherishing. He holds you close to his heart. In all his marvelous, unimaginable glory as the great King of heaven and earth, God draws near to you and gives you strength.

Do you feel forgotten? Does your life feel enfolded in difficulty, hidden from all help? Hear God's answer to you in these words. Let your Savior speak to you, and may you know the all-encompassing, ever-near love of God as you pray.

Pray:

God over all, your presence is undeserved, your peace is unmerited, and your love is unfathomable. Grant us the grace to know you as you are and to follow you all the days of our lives. For our Great Shepherd's sake. Amen.

Epiphany Day 35
STEVEN E. BREEDLOVE

Read: *Isaiah 41:21–29*

Set forth your case, says the LORD;
    bring your proofs, says the King of Jacob.
Let them bring them, and tell us
    what is to happen.
Tell us the former things, what they are,
    that we may consider them,
that we may know their outcome;
    or declare to us the things to come.
Tell us what is to come hereafter,
    that we may know that you are gods;
do good, or do harm,
    that we may be dismayed and terrified.
Behold, you are nothing,
    and your work is less than nothing;
    an abomination is he who chooses you.
I stirred up one from the north, and he has come,
    from the rising of the sun, and he shall call upon my name;
he shall trample on rulers as on mortar,
    as the potter treads clay.
Who declared it from the beginning, that we might know,
    and beforehand, that we might say, "He is right"?
There was none who declared it, none who proclaimed,
    none who heard your words.
I was the first to say to Zion, "Behold, here they are!"
    and I give to Jerusalem a herald of good news.
But when I look, there is no one;
    among these there is no counselor
    who, when I ask, gives an answer.
Behold, they are all a delusion;
    their works are nothing;
    their metal images are empty wind.

Reflect:

Isaiah 41 depicts a courtroom scene, a trial where God was both judge and prosecutor. The nations watched as God proved his case. The idols of the world were defendants prosecuted by God. Yet there was also a special group in the audience, and the trial was for their benefit: Israel.

God questioned and accused the idols in Israel's presence, challenging them to predict the future or explain the past. But he also addressed Israel directly as a prosecutor might address a jury. Israel must listen because they had depended on the idols of pagan nations many times. They had been humbled and broken by these nations, and they were fearful. Where had the God of Israel been in this dangerous world?

Yet the Lord answered their fears. He said to them, "Fear not, for I am with you; be not dismayed, for I am your God; I will strengthen you, I will help you" (Isaiah 41:10). Over and over, he told them not to fear. He had not abandoned his people. He would rescue them from slavery and exile.

God proves that the idols are nothing; they are merely things people build to protect themselves. They cannot do anything, they do not know the past, and they cannot tell the future. God alone can do these things; he alone is Lord over history, and the world is in his hands.

As you pray, consider that we, like Israel, live in a chaotic world. Like Israel, we are tempted to trust in what we build with our hands. Like Israel, we forget that God is the King of all nations, and we attempt to protect ourselves by our own efforts and power.

Pray:

You, O Lord our God, hold us by the right hand. It is you who says to us, "Fear not, I am the one who helps you!" You are the Holy One of Israel yet also our Redeemer. You alone know the future, and nothing happens outside your sight. May we live without fear, trusting that you are Lord over history. Amen.

Epiphany Day 36
STEVEN E. BREEDLOVE

Read: *Isaiah 42:1–4*

> Behold my servant, whom I uphold,
> > my chosen, in whom my soul delights;
> I have put my Spirit upon him;
> > he will bring forth justice to the nations.
> He will not cry aloud or lift up his voice,
> > or make it heard in the street;
> a bruised reed he will not break,
> > and a faintly burning wick he will not quench;
> > he will faithfully bring forth justice.
> He will not grow faint or be discouraged
> > till he has established justice in the earth;
> > and the coastlands wait for his law.

Reflect:

In the midst of God's indictment of the idols of the nations, he paused to describe his servant. The idols were nothing, unable to save and ignorant of the past and the future. Israel's God alone is the Lord—he alone can deliver, and he alone knows the future. But remarkably, even God's servant could do what the idols cannot; he would succeed in bringing justice to all nations! God has proven throughout history—through people such as Moses, Deborah, and David, and even pagans like Cyrus—that when he desires, he can anoint an ordinary person and, through this servant, bring justice and salvation. His lowly servants are more powerful than the gods of the nations, simply because the Spirit of God rests on them.

We know that God the Father is ultimately speaking of his Son, who is the true Servant of God. Anointed by the Spirit at his baptism, he has triumphed and brought justice and the law of salvation to the ends of the earth. He is the true image of God, the living icon, God himself in the flesh, and he can do what false gods cannot. But in Jesus we also see the character of the Father, who declared, "A bruised reed [a servant] will not break, and a faintly burning wick he will not quench" (v. 3). Jesus delivers with tenderness, protecting the wounded as he conquers, enlarging the faith of hearts that are only faintly burning wicks. God's character shines through the life of Jesus as he shields the bruised and fainting and accomplishes justice.

As you pray, remember that God uses his humble servants, anointed by the Spirit, to deliver. Remember that his salvation is tender, protecting those who are bruised and only faintly alive.

Let us pray that God will heal our bruises and brighten our small flames of faith.

Let us pray that we will see where he is anointing ordinary people to deliver others.

Let us pray that he will anoint us to bring justice and the law of salvation to the nations.

Pray:

O Lord, you have anointed your Son, the true Servant, to bring salvation to the world. Anoint us also with your Spirit so that we might be his messengers of salvation to the bruised reeds and faintly burning wicks who live near us. Amen.

Epiphany Day 37
STEVEN E. BREEDLOVE

Read: *Isaiah 43:1–5*

But now thus says the LORD,
he who created you, O Jacob,
he who formed you, O Israel:
"Fear not, for I have redeemed you;
I have called you by name, you are mine.
When you pass through the waters, I will be with you;
and through the rivers, they shall not overwhelm you;
when you walk through fire you shall not be burned,
and the flame shall not consume you.
For I am the LORD your God,
the Holy One of Israel, your Savior.
I give Egypt as your ransom,
Cush and Seba in exchange for you.
Because you are precious in my eyes,
and honored, and I love you,
I give men in return for you,
peoples in exchange for your life.
Fear not, for I am with you;
I will bring your offspring from the east,
and from the west I will gather you."

Reflect:

There are moments in the Bible when we see that God's concerns are not always the same as ours. We want to be free from pain, but God cares more that our hearts long for his presence and that we trust him.

God allowed his people to be plundered, trapped, and hidden in prisons because they rejected him. Judah had sinned against God and refused to walk in his ways, and so God gave his people to their enemies. They longed to be free of the exile, but God longed more for them to be faithful to him.

But even in delivering his people up to suffering and exile, God did not abandon them. His love for them was far too strong. He promised redemption, where prisoners are released to go home. God chastised for a season, but he did not abandon. It was because of his love that he purged his people of their idolatry, for idolatry brings death.

Yet even in the dark moments when God's people were driven from home, God was not far off. When Daniel's three friends were cast into the fiery furnace in Babylon, God walked there with them. Ezekiel, while in the land of Babylon, saw the throne of God carried by angels so that God would be with the exiles where they were. They were being disciplined, but God was suffering their exile with them. And in Isaiah 43:2, we hear God say to those in exile, "When you pass through the waters, I will be with you."

I will be with you. I will be with you in your suffering. I will be with you in your grief. I will be with you in your exhaustion. And even if I have to discipline you to purge you of idolatry, I will be with you in the discipline.

As you pray, rejoice that the Lord is with you no matter where you are or what you are enduring. Let us pray for those Christians who are blind to the presence of God in their lives. Let us pray for those who have not yet met God and do not know that he would be with them.

Pray:

You, O Lord, have created and formed us. You have redeemed us, so we need not fear. You have walked through the waters with us; indeed, you have walked through the waters of death for us. The flames will not destroy us, for we are called by your name! You are the Holy One of Israel, our Savior! Amen.

Epiphany Day 38
STEVEN E. BREEDLOVE

Read: *Isaiah 44:1–5*

> "But now hear, O Jacob my servant,
>   Israel whom I have chosen!
> Thus says the LORD who made you,
>   who formed you from the womb and will help you:
> Fear not, O Jacob my servant,
>   Jeshurun whom I have chosen.
> For I will pour water on the thirsty land,
>   and streams on the dry ground;
> I will pour my Spirit upon your offspring,
>   and my blessing on your descendants.
> They shall spring up among the grass
>   like willows by flowing streams.
> This one will say, 'I am the LORD's,'
>   another will call on the name of Jacob,
> and another will write on his hand, 'The LORD's,'
>   and name himself by the name of Israel."

Reflect:

One of the greatest and most frequent themes of the prophets is God's faithfulness to his people even while they are faithless to him. He is the husband pursuing his adulterous wife or the father stretching out his hands to his rebellious son. His people are perpetually wandering, going astray, and joining themselves to other lovers and masters.

In the midst of this dark night of faithlessness, Isaiah 44:5 gleams like a torch. The people finally began to understand—they were God's through and through! No more false masters, no more illicit lovers. They wrote his name on their hands, just as a child with a marker claims toys as her own. No one would ever again forget that he or she belonged to God!

But this didn't happen because the people were finally enlightened or finally faithful. Isaiah 43 ends, yet again, with the failure of the people.

The people didn't reach this point of understanding because of something in and of themselves. They weren't better than the rest. In the words of Isaiah 44:3, they were merely "thirsty land" and "dry ground." But God wasn't content for them to stay that way. He poured out his Spirit, watering their hearts and transforming them so that they finally realized who they were—God's people through and through! It was the Spirit, undeserved and without measure, poured on the thirsty land of their hearts, that caused this transformation.

As you pray, acknowledge the thirsty land of your heart. Acknowledge its dry ground.

Let us pray that God will continually pour out his Spirit on us, watering the cracked and dry ground of our hearts. Let us pray that God will pour out his Spirit in our families, so that we will believe within the depths of our being that we are the Lord's. Let us pray that God will pour out his Spirit on our churches, so that the only thing that matters to us is faithfulness to God.

Pray:

You, O Lord, have chosen us! You have formed us from the womb and helped us. You have poured water on the thirsty land of our hearts and sent streams through the desert places of our lives. Pour out your Spirit yet again so that we might know that we are yours! Amen.

Epiphany Day 39
STEVEN E. BREEDLOVE

Read: *Isaiah 45:1–7*

    Thus says the LORD to his anointed, to Cyrus,
        whose right hand I have grasped,
    to subdue nations before him
        and to loose the belts of kings,
    to open doors before him
        that gates may not be closed:
"I will go before you
        and level the exalted places,
I will break in pieces the doors of bronze
        and cut through the bars of iron,
I will give you the treasures of darkness
        and the hoards in secret places,
that you may know that it is I, the LORD,
        the God of Israel, who call you by your name.
For the sake of my servant Jacob,
        and Israel my chosen,
I call you by your name,
        I name you, though you do not know me.
I am the LORD, and there is no other,
        besides me there is no God;
        I equip you, though you do not know me,
that people may know, from the rising of the sun
        and from the west, that there is none besides me;
        I am the LORD, and there is no other.
I form light and create darkness;
        I make well-being and create calamity;
        I am the LORD, who does all these things."

Reflect:

It must have been startling to the Israelites that God was going to use Cyrus, the great Persian king, to save the Israelites. He was a pagan who did not know the God of Israel—an idol-worshipper! Was there no new Moses or faithful Israelite that the Lord could raise up to deliver his people? Why use a pagan king?

Yet God anointed him, subdued nations under him, broke the doors of bronze before him, and gave him the treasures of other nations. Israel had suffered under the great kings of pagan nations—Egypt, Assyria, Babylon—so the ascent of Cyrus must have filled them with dread.

Yet God raised up Cyrus for the sake of his servant Jacob, for Israel, his chosen one! He exalted a ruler they would never have chosen. There are many times when God does not tell his people why he does what he does, but in this instance, he explained himself. His reasoning was simple. He used a pagan king to deliver his people, one they could not control and did not expect, simply so that they might finally understand that God, and God alone, is the Lord.

If the deliverer had been one of their own, someone they could trust and control, they would always have been tempted to believe that they had played a role in their deliverance. But God desired for his people to finally say, "Only you, O Lord, create light and darkness; only you can raise up or destroy nations. Only you are God!"

As you pray, remember that God uses people we do not expect to accomplish his will. Remember that he, and he alone, can deliver.

Remember that he is the Lord over kings and nations and is Lord over the past, present, and future.

Let us pray that we will see where God is at work in our nation. Let us pray that we will grow to believe that only God can deliver. Let us pray that we will follow where God leads rather than trying to do things our way.

Pray:
Lord, thank you that you create new hearts within us. Give us the grace to be humble and to love what you love. In Christ's holy name. Amen.

Epiphany Day 40
STEVEN E. BREEDLOVE

Read: *Isaiah 46:3–7*

> "Listen to me, O house of Jacob,
>   all the remnant of the house of Israel,
> who have been borne by me from before your birth,
>   carried from the womb;
> even to your old age I am he,
>   and to gray hairs I will carry you.
> I have made, and I will bear;
>   I will carry and will save.
> To whom will you liken me and make me equal,
>   and compare me, that we may be alike?
> Those who lavish gold from the purse,
>   and weigh out silver in the scales,
> hire a goldsmith, and he makes it into a god;
>   then they fall down and worship!
> They lift it to their shoulders, they carry it,
>   they set it in its place, and it stands there;
>   it cannot move from its place.
> If one cries to it, it does not answer
>   or save him from his trouble."

Reflect:

God's prosecution of the idols is full of holy mockery. He is nothing like the gods of the nations, who are mere statues crafted by goldsmiths for a fee. People cry out to these gods for deliverance from trouble, yet the gods cannot even move themselves, let alone the people who worship them. They are so helpless that they have to be carried on the shoulders of men.

God, on the other hand, is the one carrying his people. He does what the idols cannot, and he has borne his people from cradle to grave for centuries. They rest on his secure shoulders.

176

Though we are unlikely to cry out to a statue to carry us and deliver us, we still face the temptation of seeking help from the works of our hands. We look to our careers, our bank accounts, or our political parties to assist us, deliver us, and save us. Yet like the idols of nations long destroyed, the works of our hands cannot carry us—we carry and build them. They are less powerful than we are because we created them. It makes no sense that we would trust in their power to protect us.

Only God has the strength to carry us. Only God has the strength to save us. He has held us on his shoulders since before our birth, and he will carry us beyond the grave!

As you pray, remember the times when you have felt God carrying you. Remember the moments when you have witnessed his deliverance.

Let us pray that we will not trust the works of our hands for salvation. Let us pray that we will seek refuge in the hands of our Creator.

Let us pray that we will remember that God is carrying us at every moment of every day.

Pray:

Lord, you have borne us from before our lives began, even from the womb! You will bear us until old age and the grave. You have made us; you will continue to carry us; you will save us! Amen.

(adapted from *Isaiah 46*)

Epiphany Day 41
WILLA KANE

Read: *Isaiah 47:5–7*

> Sit in silence, and go into darkness,
>   O daughter of the Chaldeans;
> for you shall no more be called
>   the mistress of kingdoms.
> I was angry with my people;
>   I profaned my heritage;
> I gave them into your hand;
>   you showed them no mercy;
> on the aged you made your yoke exceedingly heavy.
> You said, "I shall be mistress forever,"
>   so that you did not lay these things to heart
>   or remember their end.

Reflect:

Isaiah 47 is one of those passages that many people struggle to appreciate. God's rebuke of Babylon and his prophecy of judgment seem worlds away from the twenty-first century. Yet even here we hear the heart of God; even here his voice can speak to us.

As he said to Babylon, he was angry with his people, so he profaned his heritage. They had rejected him, so he sent them into exile and defiled the land. But he was not seeking to destroy them. Exile was ultimately for salvation. The idols they worshipped endangered not just their homes but their souls. God removed them from their homes to break their enslavement to idols and save their souls.

But the Babylonians were proud, and they showed no mercy to the Jews. They thought that they would rule forever and showed no regard for the weak and pitiful. So God declared that Babylon, too, would be destroyed.

God cares for the weak, the aged, and the vulnerable. Those who are poor and humble in spirit are precious to him. The proud, the merciless, and the cruel are rejected by him because they show no regard for those in whom God delights.

As you pray, take great comfort in the fact that God loves you—not because of your successes and strength but simply because he created you. He does not need you to be powerful and is not ashamed of your weakness. But as you pray, also remember that God rejects those who, in their pride, despise the weak and the humble of the world.

Let us pray that God will root out all pride and cruelty from our hearts. Let us pray that, like God, we will protect and care for the weak.

Let us pray in thanksgiving that God is near to us as we are poor in spirit and brokenhearted.

Pray:

O God, you are the Redeemer of the humble, the Savior of the weak. You reject those who arrogantly destroy others. Soften our hearts to the cries of the weak. Keep us from pride and cruelty. Thank you for loving us in our weakness! Amen.

Epiphany Day 42
ART GOING

Read: *Isaiah 48:1–6*

> Hear this, O house of Jacob,
>> who are called by the name of Israel,
>> and who came from the waters of Judah,
> who swear by the name of the LORD
>> and confess the God of Israel, but not in truth or right.
> For they call themselves after the holy city,
>> and stay themselves on the God of Israel;
>> the LORD of hosts is his name.
> "The former things I declared of old;
>> they went out from my mouth, and I announced them;
>> then suddenly I did them, and they came to pass.
> Because I know that you are obstinate,
>> and your neck is an iron sinew
>> and your forehead brass,
> I declared them to you from of old,
>> before they came to pass I announced them to you,
> lest you should say, 'My idol did them,
>> my carved image and my metal image commanded them.'
> "You have heard; now see all this;
>> and will you not declare it?
> From this time forth I announce to you new things,
>> hidden things that you have not known."

Reflect:

In the NIV translation, the first word of Isaiah 48:1 is the key: listen. Isaiah used the word ten times in this chapter, and it keeps coming back in the ensuing chapters. The Hebrew word is the familiar and essential *Shema*—the first word and name of the Jewish profession of faith (Deuteronomy 6:4): *Hear, O Israel.* Amid all the themes of these chapters of Isaiah is the recurring invitation: *listen.*

And oh, how we need to listen! Hearing a clear word from God is the only way we'll escape the prison of self and the allurement of culture. The living God speaks so that we will not listen fruitlessly to only ourselves or our cultural idols. Isaiah reprimanded Israel for not really listening to God. They confessed faith but failed to live it out.

They not only were quick to credit idols for their blessings but also were closed to the "new things" (v. 6) God had in store. And even though God had told them about his character and his mighty acts, they had never been good listeners.

That's the challenge and invitation to us: become listeners!

As you pray, ask for focus and attentiveness this season to the God who speaks, who speaks to you. Examine your listening. Take an inventory of the voices that drown out the voice that matters most—namely, that of the God who wants to do a new thing in your life.

Pray:

O Almighty God, you pour out on all who desire it the spirit of grace and of supplication: Deliver us, when we draw near to you, from coldness of heart and wanderings of mind, that with steadfast thoughts and kindled affections we may worship you in spirit and in truth; through Jesus Christ our Lord. Amen.

(Anglican Church in North America Book of Common Prayer)

Epiphany Day 43
KARI WEST

Read: *Psalm 46:1–3*

>God is our refuge and strength,
>>a very present help in trouble.
>Therefore we will not fear though the earth gives way,
>>though the mountains be moved into the heart of the sea,
>though its waters roar and foam,
>>though the mountains tremble at its swelling. *Selah*

Reflect:

Perhaps these vivid descriptions of chaos and uncertainty—the earth giving way, water roaring, and mountains quaking—strike a chord of resonance for you. Perhaps your days feel closer to calamity than calm.

What are we to do as the earth trembles and the mountains fall into the heart of the sea?

May we be a people who find fresh courage in the answer this psalm offers us. God is our constant help in every season. God is our strong refuge.

God is our Rock and our fortress. God dwells forever in his holy city, and we will one day gather on those distant shores of glory. The trials of this present time cannot compare to what lies in wait for those who are the Lord's.

As you pray, take one of the descriptions of God in this passage and meditate on it. Ask the Lord to give you fresh insight into his character. Praise him for his constancy and his care.

Pray:

Father, you are our refuge and strength,
an ever-present help in trouble.
Therefore we will not fear, though the earth give way
and the mountains fall into the heart of the sea,
though its waters roar and foam
and the mountains quake with their surging.
Lord Almighty, you are with us.
God of Jacob, you are our fortress. Amen.

(adapted from *Psalm 46*)

Epiphany Day 44
MATT HOEHN

Read: *2 Corinthians 9:7–8*

> Each one must give as he has decided in his heart, not reluctantly or under compulsion, for God loves a cheerful giver. And God is able to make all grace abound to you, so that having all sufficiency in all things at all times, you may abound in every good work.

Reflect:

When paying off monthly credit card debts, do you find it jarring to observe how many of life's expenses are obligatory and bring no sense of pleasure?

We're reminded by Paul in this passage from 2 Corinthians 9 that our tithes and offerings to Christ and his church are to be markedly different. The mark of Christian giving is cheerfulness—a deep pleasure at the opportunity to present our gifts to the Father, who created us out of love; to the Son, who gave up his life to redeem us; and to the Spirit, who resides in us and sanctifies us. Paul wrote elsewhere that "it is for freedom that Christ has set us free" from the works of the law (Galatians 5:1 NIV), and these verses in 2 Corinthians remind us that this freedom pertains to giving as well. We are to give not out of reluctant obligation but out of gratitude for all that God has given to us. We are to give not out of begrudging compulsion but out of a genuine desire.

While we don't give out of a utilitarian expectation of return, Paul did promise that God gives good gifts to the cheerful giver—namely, God's love, his abounding grace in one's life, all of life's needs being sufficiently met, and being equipped for good works. The Christian gives cheerfully because God is a benevolent God—he has already given us the greatest possible gift of his own Son, and he will not be frugal in giving us these additional good gifts as well.

As you pray, consider your recent heart posture toward giving and tithing. Have you been reluctant? Have you felt under compulsion? Or has giving been an occasion of joy for you?

Pray:

Almighty God, you are the Maker of all things and Lord over all creation. We ask that you give us cheerful hearts in returning to you a portion of all that you have given to us, so that our hearts may be aligned with your will. We ask this through Jesus Christ your Son, your ultimate gift, given to us out of love. Amen.

Epiphany Day 45
MATT HOEHN

Read: *2 Corinthians 10:3–6*

> For though we walk in the flesh, we are not waging war according
> to the flesh. For the weapons of our warfare are not of the flesh but
> have divine power to destroy strongholds. We destroy arguments
> and every lofty opinion raised against the knowledge of God, and
> take every thought captive to obey Christ, being ready to punish
> every disobedience, when your obedience is complete.

Reflect:

"Be in the world but not of the world" is a familiar saying in Christian circles. It means we are dual citizens. We are temporarily residents of this world, and we are called to inhabit it in a faithful way. However, our ultimate home is in the kingdom of God, and this kingdom commands our truest allegiance.

"Being in the world" as Christians often entails opposition—being on the receiving end of misunderstandings, slights, and sometimes even overt antipathy. Paul reminded us that this battle is spiritual in nature and not simply according to the flesh. As citizens of the kingdom of God whose allegiance is to Christ, we are not to condescend to the "battle tactics" of this world: insults, slander, incendiary social media retorts, or a "punch back" mentality. We are to fight this battle with entirely different weaponry—the armor of God (Ephesians 6:10–20), which includes the belt of truth, the breastplate of righteousness, the shield of faith, and the sword of the Spirit.

Though the world may revile us and throw its worst at us, our fight is not aimed at the destruction of our perceived opponents, but at their salvation. We are to wield our spiritual weapons to "destroy arguments and every lofty opinion raised against the knowledge of God" (2 Corinthians 10:5). The first subject of our weaponry is ourselves. We are to discipline ourselves to "take every thought captive to obey Christ" (v. 5).

It can be tempting to lower our standards to the world's standards of combat when defending the faith—to adopt an "ends justify the means" mentality. Paul would have none of this. We must always keep at the forefront of our minds that "we are not waging war according to the flesh" (v. 3) and "the weapons of our warfare are not of the flesh" (v. 4).

Prayer is perhaps the leading weapon with "divine power to destroy strongholds" (v. 4). As you pray, ask that God would equip you to die to self, live for Christ, and oppose Satan, sin, and temptation in all that you do.

Pray:
Grant me, O Lord, to know what I ought to know,
to love what I ought to love,
to praise what delights thee most,
to value what is precious in thy sight,
to hate what is offensive to thee.
Do not suffer me to judge according to the sight
    of my eyes,
nor to pass sentence according to the hearing
    of the ears of ignorant men;
but to discern with a true judgment between things
    visible and spiritual,
and above all, always to inquire what is the good
    pleasure of thy will. Amen.

(Thomas à Kempis)

Epiphany Day 46
SALLY BREEDLOVE

Read: *2 Corinthians 11:2–3*

> For I feel a divine jealousy for you, since I betrothed you to one
> husband, to present you as a pure virgin to Christ. But I am afraid
> that as the serpent deceived Eve by his cunning, your thoughts will
> be led astray from a sincere and pure devotion to Christ.

Reflect:

When we think of the virtues that comprise the Christian life and the corre-
sponding vices that tempt us, we tend to classify jealousy among the latter.
Wasn't jealousy the second-ever recorded sin in the Bible, the motivation that
led Cain to murder his brother Abel? Isn't "You shall not covet" one of the
Ten Commandments?

But jealousy can have two senses—a negative and fleshly one and a posi-
tive and spiritual one. In these verses from 2 Corinthians, Paul expressed a
divine jealousy for this flock of Christians he had shepherded, yearning that
they would continue walking earnestly in the faith and not be "led astray
from a sincere and pure devotion to Christ" (v. 3).

Like the men and women of the Corinthian church, we are all made in
the image of God and designed for a relationship with him. While Satan has
tried to claim us as his own through the power of sin, the work of Christ
on the cross has restored us to the Father. "He has delivered us from the
domain of darkness and transferred us to the kingdom of his beloved Son"
(Colossians 1:13). It is good and right to feel a divine jealousy toward fellow
believers, a possessive zeal to remind our brothers and sisters of who they are
and whose they are.

The same God who commands us not to covet in the tenth commandment also says in the second commandment, "You shall not bow down to
[any other gods] or serve them, for I the LORD your God am a jealous God"
(Exodus 20:5). Elsewhere in Exodus, God reveals that the divine name is

even synonymous with jealousy: "You shall worship no other God, for the LORD, whose name is Jealous, is a jealous God" (Exodus 34:14).

While jealousy of our neighbor's belongings is sinful, jealousy for our neighbor's continuation in the faith is godly. As you pray, ask the Lord to give you a proper divine jealousy for your fellow brothers and sisters in Christ.

Pray:

Almighty God, you created us out of love, and we belong to you. Your zeal for us to know and love you is great, and your desire for us not to be led astray by the deceit of sin is absolute. Cleanse us from our petty worldly jealousies and replace them with a proper divine jealousy for our fellow man and fellow woman to know you. All this we ask by the powerful name of Jesus, the supreme demonstration of your perfect jealous love for us. Amen.

Epiphany Day 47
MATT HOEHN

Read: *2 Corinthians 12:7–10*

So to keep me from becoming conceited because of the surpassing greatness of the revelations, a thorn was given me in the flesh, a messenger of Satan to harass me, to keep me from becoming conceited. Three times I pleaded with the Lord about this, that it should leave me. But he said to me, "My grace is sufficient for you, for my power is made perfect in weakness." Therefore I will boast all the more gladly of my weaknesses, so that the power of Christ may rest upon me. For the sake of Christ, then, I am content with weaknesses, insults, hardships, persecutions, and calamities. For when I am weak, then I am strong.

Reflect:

While the Bible is clear on the fundamentals, or "all things necessary for salvation," such as the character of God, the plight of sinful humankind, and the saving work of Christ, it also leaves many questions unanswered relating to tertiary issues.

Our passage today raises one such question: What was Paul's thorn in the flesh? We simply don't know. Paul didn't reveal the specifics to us here or elsewhere. While we can't know what Paul's thorn was, we can all relate to it. Following Adam's fall, all of us are afflicted in various ways. All of us have things in our lives—thought patterns, sinful inclinations, marred relationships—that we long for God to destroy or redeem. Adam chose sin and tainted the human condition for all, and now we all have hurts, habits, and hang-ups that beset our lives.

While Paul had previously repeatedly implored the Lord to remove this thorn, he later came to see that God had a purpose in it. Our thorns remind us of our true condition, sinful and frail, and rid us of our proclivities toward conceit and pride. Our thorns remind us that we are not in control of our own lives and are not our own saviors. We desperately need the power of

Christ in our lives. Our thorns provide an opportunity for us to taste and see that God's grace is our portion. It is sufficient for us, regardless of our circumstances or struggles.

As you pray, bring to mind a thorn from your life and present it to the Lord. Rather than asking exclusively that he would remove it, pray that the Lord would use whatever the affliction, ailment, or circumstance may be to demonstrate his power in the midst of your weakness.

Pray:

Almighty God, whose most dear Son went not up to joy but first he suffered pain, and entered not into glory before he was crucified: Mercifully grant that we, walking in the way of the Cross, may find it none other than the way of life and peace; through Jesus Christ our Lord. Amen.

(Anglican Church in North America Book of Common Prayer)

Epiphany Day 48

MATT HOEHN

Read: *2 Corinthians 13:11–14*

> Finally, brothers, rejoice. Aim for restoration, comfort one another, agree with one another, live in peace; and the God of love and peace will be with you. Greet one another with a holy kiss. All the saints greet you.
>
> The grace of the Lord Jesus Christ and the love of God and the fellowship of the Holy Spirit be with you all.

Reflect:

When reading one of Paul's letters, one may find it tempting to gloss over the valediction, the parting farewell, and the final instructions to the letter's recipients.

But the conclusion of the epistle is crucially important and often captures the essence of Paul's heart, as is the case with 2 Corinthians. Throughout this letter, Paul laid out a vision for how the church at Corinth should follow Christ communally as one body. Here at the close, Paul hammered home this theme with three "one another" exhortations: comfort one another, agree with one another, and greet one another with affection. Christians are not to be those who obstinately insist on their way to the point of division and disunity; they are to be those who "aim for restoration" and "live in peace" (v. 11).

In our day and age where individuality is valorized and submission to a community is thought ludicrous, we would do well to heed Paul's instructions. We Christians should be known as a people whose corporate life together is characterized by restoration, mutual comfort, agreement, and peace.

As you pray, ask the Lord for unity in the body of Christ—in your immediate relationships, at your home congregation, and throughout the wider global church.

Pray:

Almighty God, you sent your Son Jesus to purchase his bride, the Church, with his own shed blood. In spite of its defects, you see the Church as radiant and clothed in the righteousness of your Son. Grant your Church to have the mind of Christ among its many members so that we may be knit together in love, concord, and peace, and so the watching world may know you through your Church. Amen.

Epiphany Day 49
KARI WEST

Read: *Romans 1:1–7*

> Paul, a servant of Christ Jesus, called to be an apostle, set apart
> for the gospel of God, which he promised beforehand through
> his prophets in the holy Scriptures, concerning his Son, who was
> descended from David according to the flesh and was declared to be
> the Son of God in power according to the Spirit of holiness by his
> resurrection from the dead, Jesus Christ our Lord, through whom
> we have received grace and apostleship to bring about the obedience
> of faith for the sake of his name among all the nations, including
> you who are called to belong to Jesus Christ,
>
> To all those in Rome who are loved by God and called to be
> saints: Grace to you and peace from God our Father and the Lord
> Jesus Christ.

Reflect:

What comes to mind when you think about the gospel? Is it primarily an intellectual concept, a list of theological ideas, a rubric for moral living, a half-remembered story from your churched childhood?

Hear how Paul described the good news in this passage: what God has done *for us.*

This long-promised reality of the Son of God clothing himself in humanity, living perfectly, dying sacrificially, and resurrecting in power—it was all done by God so we could belong to him. We who hated him, we who ran from him, we who had nothing to offer to our Creator God, we who would die in our miserable rebellion—now we are the friends of God.

Why did Christ live, die, and return to life? Paul knew—it was so God could give us grace and peace.

God did everything for us so that we could be his own.

As you pray, meditate on this passage and ask the Spirit to reveal the deep, personal, intimate love of your Father for you in these words. You are his, and he has moved heaven and earth to make it so.

Pray:

Father, may you give us the strength to comprehend with all the saints what is the breadth and length and height and depth, and to know the love of Christ that surpasses knowledge, that we may be filled with all the fullness of you. Amen.

(adapted from Ephesians 3:18–19)

Epiphany Day 50
MATT HOEHN

Read: *Romans 1:16–17*

> For I am not ashamed of the gospel, for it is the power of God for salvation to everyone who believes, to the Jew first and also to the Greek. For in it the righteousness of God is revealed from faith for faith, as it is written, "The righteous shall live by faith."

Reflect:

We are regularly faced with circumstances where it would be easier to downplay our commitment to Christ. Whether a business situation where colleagues of ours are cutting corners, a social setting that has devolved into gossip, or a classroom context where the teaching of the instructor is confrontational toward a biblically shaped outlook, sometimes our faith can call us to live in ways that are inconvenient, socially awkward, and personally costly.

Paul's declaration in Romans 1:16 serves as a booming cannon of encouragement to us when facing such circumstances. "For I am not ashamed of the gospel, for it is the power of God for salvation to everyone who believes, to the Jew first and also to the Greek." While it can be tempting in certain scenarios to shrink from our discipleship, we are called to be boldly unashamed of our identity in Christ.

The gospel reveals the righteousness of God—his covenant faithfulness to his promises and his perfect and holy character, which covers our sin and shame. While we are not righteous by our own natural inclination, we receive the very righteousness of God as a gift through faith in Christ, the "Righteous One" (Acts 3:14).

Jesus said in Luke 9:26, "For whoever is ashamed of me and of my words, of him will the Son of Man be ashamed when he comes in his glory and the glory of the Father and of the holy angels."

These verses from today's passage in Romans remind us that whatever the circumstance may be, our allegiance to Christ is ultimate. As you pray, ask for grace to live not for the approval of humankind but with your eyes on the prize of salvation and the gift of Christ's righteousness, granted to you by faith.

Pray:

O God our King, by the resurrection of your Son Jesus Christ on the first day of the week, you conquered sin, put death to flight, and gave us the hope of everlasting life: Redeem all our days by this victory; forgive our sins, banish our fears, make us bold to praise you and to do your will; and steel us to wait for the consummation of your kingdom on the last great Day; through Jesus Christ our Lord. Amen.

(Anglican Church in North America Book of Common Prayer)

Epiphany Day 51
MATT HOEHN

Read: *Romans 2:1–4*

> Therefore you have no excuse, O man, every one of you who judges.
> For in passing judgment on another you condemn yourself, because
> you, the judge, practice the very same things. We know that the
> judgment of God rightly falls on those who practice such things.
> Do you suppose, O man—you who judge those who practice such
> things and yet do them yourself—that you will escape the judg-
> ment of God? Or do you presume on the riches of his kindness and
> forbearance and patience, not knowing that God's kindness is meant
> to lead you to repentance?

Reflect:

One of the most moving, powerful, and dramatic scenes of the entire Old
Testament took place when the prophet Nathan confronted King David
about his sin with Bathsheba and his murder of her husband, Uriah. David
was so blinded by his own sin that Nathan intuited that the only way to get
through to him was to set a rhetorical trap.

Desiring to evoke a visceral reaction from David, Nathan told a parable
of a wealthy owner of many sheep who stole the lone beloved sheep of a poor
man. David "burned with anger" and rashly declared, "As surely as the LORD
lives, the man who did this must die!" Without missing a beat, Nathan stared
David straight in the eye and issued a shocking rebuke: "You are the man!"
(2 Samuel 12:5–7 NIV).

According to Romans 2, Nathan's rebuke was also aimed at all of us. All
of us "have no excuse" for our sinfulness, because we pass judgment on others
and then fail to live up to the standards of our own judging. All of us are
beset by hypocrisy. We are condemned by the very standards we establish for
others. If you can't escape your own judgment, Paul rightly questioned, "Do
you suppose . . . that you will escape the judgment of God?" (v. 3).

198

Graciously, God provides a means of escape from both our hypocrisy and his judgment in the riches of his kindness, forbearance, and patience, all of which lead us to repentance. Rather than our hypocrisy caging us in shame, it serves as a reminder that there is a just Judge with a perfect standard of justice. Though we fail to meet his standard, the Judge has also become the judged and has absorbed the blow of his own justice in our place. Through repentance of our sin and placing our faith in him, our souls find forgiveness and our consciences find peace.

As you pray, consider that Nathan's rebuke of David is true of you as well. Read God's kindness, forbearance, and patience in not judging you according to your own fickle standards but rather sending his Son to be judged according to God's perfect standard in your place.

Pray:

O God, the strength of all who put their trust in you: Mercifully accept our prayers, and because, through the weakness of our mortal nature, we can do no good thing without you, grant us the help of your grace to keep your commandments, that we may please you in will and deed; through Jesus Christ our Lord, who lives and reigns with you and the Holy Spirit, one God, for ever and ever. Amen.

(Anglican Church in North America Book of Common Prayer)

Epiphany Day 52
MADISON PERRY

Read: *Romans 5:1–5*

> Therefore, since we have been justified by faith, we have peace with
> God through our Lord Jesus Christ. Through him we have also
> obtained access by faith into this grace in which we stand, and we
> rejoice in hope of the glory of God. Not only that, but we rejoice
> in our sufferings, knowing that suffering produces endurance, and
> endurance produces character, and character produces hope, and
> hope does not put us to shame, because God's love has been poured
> into our hearts through the Holy Spirit who has been given to us.

Reflect:

Paul's assertions startle us. Suffering leads to good things? Endurance
improves our character? A person of character knows real, solid hope?

If we are honest, we know suffering can be good for us, but we prefer to
find a way around it or to fight against it. How much easier it is to want life
to be carefree and to hope in vanishing, temporary things!

But in times of distress, we have the opportunity to be made strong by
God, to learn to hope in the things that last, and, best of all, to find the love
of God being poured into our hearts in new ways.

As you pray, ask God to help you embrace your life as it is right now.
Ask him to help you know the solid ground of his peace and grace. Think of
someone else who is experiencing troubles, and pray for that person, asking
that he or she would know courage and hope because of the grace and peace
of the Lord Jesus Christ.

Pray:

O Lord, support us all the day long through this trouble-filled life, until the shadows lengthen, and the evening comes, and the busy world is hushed, and the fever of life is over, and our work is done. Then in your mercy grant us a safe lodging, and a holy rest, and peace at the last. Amen.

(John Henry Newman)

Epiphany Day 53
MARY RACHEL BOYD

Read: *Romans 5:17–19*

> For if, because of one man's trespass, death reigned through that one man, much more will those who receive the abundance of grace and the free gift of righteousness reign in life through the one man Jesus Christ.
>
> Therefore, as one trespass led to condemnation for all men, so one act of righteousness leads to justification and life for all men. For as by the one man's disobedience the many were made sinners, so by the one man's obedience the many will be made righteous.

Reflect:

Paul was speaking in this passage to an audience who understood the law as a check on sinful human impulse. Indeed, it's easy for most of us to think that keeping the right rules will earn us good standing with God. But Paul pointed us away from our own efforts. He longed for us to see what the perfect obedience of Jesus has accomplished.

Because of Christ's obedience all the way to the cross, we are offered the free gift of righteousness. That gift doesn't just make us good; it frees us to be fully alive, to "reign in life" (v. 17), as Paul put it. No matter how robust our intentions for good have been and no matter how deep our sin, God's grace in Jesus is abundantly larger and deeper. Christ himself is our redemption, not our adherence to the law.

This pushes against our tendency to be individualistic and self-sustaining. Through Adam's disobedience, all were made sinners. There are no exceptions. However, through the coming and crucifixion of Jesus Christ (the second Adam), the tables are turned. Our perfect, obedient, righteous King bestows the gift of grace on us, the unworthy. In this mercy through Christ, we are made righteous and, as heirs of the kingdom, given the grace that reigns through righteousness, leading to eternal life.

Truly *receiving* this gift is an active thing. It demands from us a full-hearted response, an engagement on a physical, spiritual, and emotional level.

As you pray, listen for God's invitation to respond to his love. He longs for you to know the abundance of his grace; he longs for you to "reign in life"; he longs for you to be free of the burden of trying to earn righteousness on your own.

Pray:

O Father God, give me a heart to say yes to all that you want to give me in Jesus Christ. Amen.

Epiphany Day 54
MARY RACHEL BOYD

Read: *Romans 8:37–39*

No, in all these things we are more than conquerors through him who loved us. For I am sure that neither death nor life, nor angels nor rulers, nor things present nor things to come, nor powers, nor height nor depth, nor anything else in all creation, will be able to separate us from the love of God in Christ Jesus our Lord.

Reflect:

God has declared it to be true: nothing in all creation can separate us from the love of God in Christ Jesus our Lord! We are secure no matter what happens to us and no matter how we fail. But that is not all. Because Christ has offered us his perfect, rightly ordered loyal love, we can offer that genuine and steadfast love to each other.

To be able to turn outward in joy and treat others with a similar quality of faithful love, we must draw from the deep well of Christ's love for us. His Spirit longs to fill us with a love that will not run dry.

With an open mind and open heart, ponder what the power of the Holy Spirit is able to do in you and for you. Trust God: He who began a good work in you will bring it to completion. Don't be afraid: He has known you from the beginning of time. He knows where you have been and what lies ahead of you. He is mighty, just, and an ever-faithful friend.

As you pray, thank your Father for how secure you really are in Jesus. Then ask him to show you how you can love others well out of that security.

Pray:

O Father, I am kept by your love. Work that love so deeply into my whole being that I am able to love others with a steadfast and loyal love. For Christ's sake. Amen.

Epiphany Day 55
WILLA KANE

Read: *Romans 9:1–8*

I am speaking the truth in Christ—I am not lying; my conscience bears me witness in the Holy Spirit—that I have great sorrow and unceasing anguish in my heart. For I could wish that I myself were accursed and cut off from Christ for the sake of my brothers, my kinsmen according to the flesh. They are Israelites, and to them belong the adoption, the glory, the covenants, the giving of the law, the worship, and the promises. To them belong the patriarchs, and from their race, according to the flesh, is the Christ, who is God over all, blessed forever. Amen.

But it is not as though the word of God has failed. For not all who are descended from Israel belong to Israel, and not all are children of Abraham because they are his offspring, but "Through Isaac shall your offspring be named." This means that it is not the children of the flesh who are the children of God, but the children of the promise are counted as offspring.

Reflect:

In Romans 9, Paul's grief that his kinsmen were lost followed the great and glorious promises of Romans 8. Why this unexpected juxtaposition of high to low, great joy to great sorrow?

He did this to highlight a critical question for believers: How can we trust that God's promises will hold for us if we question his faithfulness to his chosen people? If they are cut off from the Savior, how can we trust the anthem of promises just sung across the verses of Romans 8?

Paul gave an emphatic answer: "It is not as though the word of God has failed" (v. 6). But this response leads to another question: What kind of children belong in God's family as his true offspring—children of flesh or children of promise?

Finding this answer sends us back to Genesis. God had promised old Abraham that barren Sarah would bear a son with descendants as numerous as the stars. In impatience or disbelief that God could do what he promised, Sarah and Abraham turned from faith to flesh, to the handmaid Hagar. The result was not a child conceived supernaturally but a child conceived in human flesh. Even so, God honored his promise, and Isaac was born "not of blood nor of the will of the flesh nor of the will of man, but of God" (John 1:13). Isaac was the child of the promise.

As you pray, examine your heart. Is there an area where you are trusting human devices for an answer to God's promises? Is impatience for his timing or unbelief in his ability to meet your need an excuse to operate in your flesh? Have you trusted in the work of Christ as your personal Savior, or are you trying to work your way to salvation? Are you a child of the flesh or a child of the promise?

Jesus is both promise and promise keeper. If you belong to Christ, then you are "Abraham's offspring, heirs according to promise" (Galatians 3:28–29). As you pray, put your whole trust in him.

Pray:

Lord God,

Take me to the cross to seek glory from its infamy;

Strip me of every pleasing pretense of righteousness

by my own doings.

O gracious Redeemer, I have neglected thee too long,

often crucified thee,

crucified thee afresh by my impenitence, put thee to open shame.

I thank thee for the patience that has borne with me so long

and for the grace that now makes me willing to be thine.

O unite me to thyself with inseparable bonds,

that nothing may ever draw me back from thee,

my Lord, my Saviour.

Amen.

(from The Valley of Vision*)*

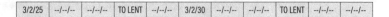

Epiphany Day 56
WILLA KANE

Read: *Romans 10:1–10*

Brothers, my heart's desire and prayer to God for them is that they
may be saved. For I bear them witness that they have a zeal for
God, but not according to knowledge. For, being ignorant of the
righteousness of God, and seeking to establish their own, they did
not submit to God's righteousness. For Christ is the end of the law
for righteousness to everyone who believes.

For Moses writes about the righteousness that is based on the
law, that the person who does the commandments shall live by them.
But the righteousness based on faith says, "Do not say in your heart,
'Who will ascend into heaven?'" (that is, to bring Christ down) "or
'Who will descend into the abyss?'" (that is, to bring Christ up
from the dead). But what does it say? "The word is near you, in
your mouth and in your heart" (that is, the word of faith that we
proclaim); because, if you confess with your mouth that Jesus is
Lord and believe in your heart that God raised him from the dead,
you will be saved. For with the heart one believes and is justified,
and with the mouth one confesses and is saved.

Reflect:

Salvation—nothing less!

Is this your desire for those separated from Christ? Do you want this
with all your heart and pray for it all the time? If you're honest, you will see
that you fall short of this standard set by Paul, whose heart beat constantly
for the lost.

We live in a world where self-concocted "salvation shops" and "noisy
knockoffs" are everywhere we turn. "You do you" is the acceptable mantra for
finding purpose and peace. Rather than taking God at his word and believing
he alone can set things right in lives that are perpetually intrinsically wrong,
people create lives on their own terms. They incur insurmountable debt to

manufactured saviors who cannot save. Even those "impressively energetic regarding God" (Romans 10:1–3 MSG) get it wrong without Jesus.

Paul made it clear in this passage that God's Word saves. God's saving grace—the incarnate Word—is Jesus. Christ, the Word that saves, is right here, as near as your next breath.

All you must do is speak a word of welcome to the God who saves. Everything that is necessary has already been done. Jesus died, was raised, was exalted, and now reigns as Lord.

Who do you know who needs to hear, receive, and accept this gospel truth? Who needs to say the word of welcome to Jesus? Pray the Lord will give you a heart that aches for those who are lost and opportunities to share this simple, life-altering truth: "If you confess with your mouth that Jesus is Lord and believe in your heart that God raised him from the dead, you will be saved. For with the heart one believes and is justified, and with the mouth one confesses and is saved" (vv. 9–10).

Pray:

Merciful God, creator of all the peoples of the earth and lover of souls: Have compassion on all who do not know you as you are revealed in your Son Jesus Christ; let your Gospel be preached with grace and power to those who have not heard it; turn the hearts of those who resist it; and bring home to your fold those who have gone astray; that there may be one flock under one Shepherd, Jesus Christ our Lord. Amen.

(Anglican Church in North America Book of Common Prayer)

Epiphany Day 57
WILLA KANE

Read: *Romans 11:1–6*

> I ask, then, has God rejected his people? By no means! For I myself
> am an Israelite, a descendant of Abraham, a member of the tribe
> of Benjamin. God has not rejected his people whom he foreknew.
> Do you not know what the Scripture says of Elijah, how he appeals
> to God against Israel? "Lord, they have killed your prophets, they
> have demolished your altars, and I alone am left, and they seek my
> life." But what is God's reply to him? "I have kept for myself seven
> thousand men who have not bowed the knee to Baal." So too at
> the present time there is a remnant, chosen by grace. But if it is by
> grace, it is no longer on the basis of works; otherwise grace would
> no longer be grace.

Reflect:

Facing a struggle that seems bigger than we are makes us feel small and alone.
Elijah experienced this loneliness nine hundred years before Christ. We feel
this today as we are increasingly confronted by those who reject or ignore
Jesus in a culture that may oppose our influence. As Paul looked back to
Elijah and into his own life, he shined an encouraging light into our present
darkness.

Here in Romans, Paul asked if God would reject his people, Israel. His
emphatic "No!" rests on personal experience—he was a Jew from the tribe of
Benjamin, yet he had not been rejected. He belonged to Christ. His response
rested on God's exchange with Elijah, alone and hiding in fear, when God
said, "I have kept for myself seven thousand who have not bowed the knee
to Baal" (v. 4). Paul's answer rested on God's promise: "So too at the present
time there is a remnant, chosen by grace" (v. 5). If you are a follower of Jesus,
this promise is also for you.

These words from our God are intensely personal. As you pray, is this the
way you see yourself? Kept by God the Father for himself?

God has always preserved a remnant. In the world's economy, remnants end up on a scrap heap. But in God's economy, his remnant is chosen, treasured, beloved, and kept.

This passage tells us clearly the way God chooses his remnant. He chooses not by works or by merit or at random, but by grace. God's grace weaves a remnant thread from the Old Testament to the New, through the lives of patriarchs, an ark builder, and a wall builder, to fishermen, prostitutes, and lepers, all the way to a Jesus-persecutor on the road to Damascus. If you are a follower of Jesus, then this remnant thread weaves through your life as well.

As you pray, thank our God that you are not alone. Thank him that your place in the glorious tapestry he is weaving with his remnant is not dependent on works but is an extravagant gift of grace.

Pray:

Almighty God our Savior, you desire that none should perish, and you have taught us through your Son that there is great joy in heaven over every sinner who repents: Grant that our hearts may ache for a lost and broken world. May your Holy Spirit work through our words, deeds, and prayers, that the lost may be found and the dead made alive, and that all your redeemed may rejoice around your throne; through Jesus Christ our Lord. Amen.

(Anglican Church in North America Book of Common Prayer)

Epiphany Day 58
WILLA KANE

Read: *Romans 12:1–2*

> I appeal to you therefore, brothers, by the mercies of God, to present your bodies as a living sacrifice, holy and acceptable to God, which is your spiritual worship. Do not be conformed to this world, but be transformed by the renewal of your mind, that by testing you may discern what is the will of God, what is good and acceptable and perfect.

Reflect:

A living sacrifice. This is what the Lord desires of us. It is what he deserves from us. In light of all the mercies God has poured out on us and for us, we take the life he has given us—body, mind, and soul—and offer it back to him for his glory and his purposes. This is possible only as our life philosophy stops conforming to the world as the Lord transforms our minds.

Paul's call to be a living sacrifice followed fifteen hundred years of a sacrificial system that led to death, not life. Those sacrifices couldn't save, but they pointed to one who could. One afternoon on a hill outside the city, Jesus, the perfect Lamb of God, changed everything.

Jesus's death defeated sin and opened the way to new life flooded with an incomprehensible list of mercies—God-given things we don't deserve. As you pray, stop to consider the mercies God has poured out for you: divine love, faith to believe, peace, patience, forgiveness, hope, the Holy Spirit, eternal life, adoption, security, comfort, and power.

A mind focused on these gifts can't focus on the world and its counterfeit treasures. Jesus died to make you his treasure. Have you died to yourself and allowed him to be yours?

We worship what we treasure. If Jesus is your treasure, then your reasonable response is to live a life of worship toward him. Living in mercy toward others, giving life away sacrificially because Jesus gave himself for you, is a life of worship. This kind of merciful living grows out of God's mercies.

All around us people need mercy. Ask the Lord where and to whom you might extend mercy. Ask for his eyes, ears, and heart to see, hear, and love the least, the lost, and the broken—mothers, fathers, sisters and brothers, children, neighbors, and strangers. See them in their need and respond with mercy. Follow Jesus in this sacrificial way of living. Place yourself as a living sacrifice on the altar of God's love.

Pray:
O God,
Fill the garden of my soul with the wind of love,
that the scents of Christian life may be wafted to others;
then come and gather fruits to thy glory.
So shall I fulfill the great end of my being—
To glorify Thee and be a blessing to men. Amen.

(from The Valley of Vision)

Epiphany Day 59
WILLA KANE

Read: *Romans 13:11–12*

> Besides this you know the time, that the hour has come for you to wake from sleep. For salvation is nearer to us now than when we first believed. The night is far gone; the day is at hand. So then let us cast off the works of darkness and put on the armor of light.

Reflect:

The apostle Paul issued a wake-up call to believers in these verses from Romans 13. He said, "You know the time, that the hour has come for you to wake from sleep" (v. 11).

The dawning of a new day calls us to wake up. The sun's rays creep over the edge of the morning horizon, first casting a glow, then banishing darkness as night becomes day. The Son who brought salvation banishes darkness for those who believe as he ushers them from the dominion of darkness into his kingdom, the kingdom of light.

If you've been ushered from darkness to light, if a new day has dawned in your heart, why do some days still feel so dark? If Jesus's death and resurrection saved once for all, then how can salvation be nearer now than when you first believed?

Salvation is a process with past, present, and future realities. Past salvation deals with sin's penalty. Present salvation deals with sin's power. Future salvation deals with sin's presence. It is this future salvation that is "nearer to us now than when we first believed" (v. 11), when Christ will return to make all things new and to gather his people to himself. Until then, we will experience darkness in a world infected by sin, even though its power over us has been broken.

Past salvation and present salvation work together in hearts, minds, and bodies by the Holy Spirit to defeat the power of sin and prepare us for that day when we will see Jesus face-to-face. Because we've been forgiven in Christ and are being refined by the Spirit, we can cast off the works of darkness and live for the gospel, protected by the armor of light. Paul described this armor as "the breastplate of faith and love, and ... a helmet the hope of salvation" (1 Thessalonians 5:8). The armor of light is faith, hope, and love.

As you pray, cast off darkness and put on the armor of light. Put on faith in the Lord Jesus Christ. Put on hope in the Lord Jesus Christ. Put on love for the Lord Jesus Christ. Clothed in him, you should answer his wake-up call. The night is far gone; the day is at hand.

Pray:

Hasten, O Father, the coming of your kingdom; and grant that we your servants, who now live by faith, may with joy behold your Son at his coming in glorious majesty; even Jesus Christ, our only Mediator and Advocate. Amen.

(Anglican Church in North America Book of Common Prayer)

Acknowledgments

*E*IGHTH DAY PRAYERS has been the work of friends coming from a cross section of people, organizations, and churches who hope in the power of Scripture-focused prayer and hunger for the growth of God's church. This prayer guide would not be in print without Willa Kane's faith, generosity, and her ability to call people to action; Madison Perry's leadership, vision, and energy; Sally Breedlove's depth of spiritual insight and writing ability; and Kari West's love for Scripture and the written word.

But these four were not adequate for the work they felt called to. Cassie Lawrence offered her gift of meticulous copy editing, Isabel Yates brought an imagination for beauty and graphic design, and Alysia Yates took this project in hand with her immense skills as an editor and her ability to see the whole.

Eighth Day Prayers began with a simple idea that would have been impossible to execute without the enlivening help of the Holy Spirit. A friend of Willa's asked her if there was a way to call people to pray for eight minutes every night at 8:00 p.m. In 2020 our world was in a crisis of fear, isolation, and confusion, so how could a dream that big come into being? Willa, Madison, and Sally did the simple things. They named and set up a website and posted daily invitations to pray. From the beginning they realized prayer that flowed from reflection on Scripture had the power to draw people to the heart of God. They wrote the first 150 or so calls to prayer, and a growing number of people joined in online.

Out of that online worldwide community of over fourteen thousand people, the idea of a book began to emerge. And more people began to help with this project. Francis Capitanio gave significant creative direction, recommending the seasonal ordering and writing several entries along the way. Other writers for this volume include Nathan Baxter, Mary Rachel Boyd, Steven A. Breedlove, Steven E. Breedlove, Elizabeth Gatewood, Art Going, Matt Hoehn, Tamara Hill Murphy, Abigail Hull Whitehouse, and Drew Williams. Steven E. Breedlove also provided the rich introductions to the Christian year and the introductions to each season. Stephen Macchia graciously provided our introduction to what it means to reflect on Scripture in a prayer-filled way. The North Carolina Study Center, a Christian Study Center based in Chapel Hill, North Carolina, devoted organizational assistance to bless the global church.

Psalm 110:3 tells us that God's people volunteer or offer themselves freely on the day of God's power. In the creation of *Eighth Day Prayers*, the triune God has indeed been our King, and his people have freely offered themselves in service. We are grateful.

About the Authors

Willa Kane is a former trustee of The Anglican Relief and Development Fund and is presently a trustee of the American Anglican Council. She is the one of the founders of New City Fellows, Raleigh, and a trustee for the ministries of Anne Graham Lotz. She was personally discipled by the late Michael Green in relational evangelism and in a commitment to care for the renewal and protection of the gospel on the global stage. For years, she has taught the Bible to women and mentored them. Together with her husband, John, she has poured her life into community leadership and development. Willa is a mother to four and a grandmother to twelve. She lives in Raleigh, NC.

Sally Breedlove is the author of *Choosing Rest* and one of the authors of *The Shame Exchange*. She is the co-founder of JourneyMates, a Christian soul care and spiritual formation ministry. She serves as a spiritual director and retreat leader and is the associate director of Selah-Anglican, a spiritual direction training program. With her husband, Steve, a bishop in the Anglican Church in North America, she has ministered broadly across the United States, in Canada, and overseas. Sally is a mother to five and a grandmother to sixteen. She lives in Chapel Hill, NC.

Madison Perry is the founder and executive director of the North Carolina Study Center, a Christian study center at UNC. He studied theology at Duke and law at UNC. An ordained priest in the Anglican Church in North America, his heart is to see university communities glorify the Lord and become places where young people are brought into God's kingdom, healed, and formed by the power of Jesus. Madison and his wife, Pamela, have six children and live in Durham, NC. He enjoys talking while walking and reading all kinds of literature.

Alysia Yates is a writer, editor, and mother of four. She earned her graduate degree in church history and currently works as the project manager for Caritas Foundation International. Alysia has served as an ESL teacher within the refugee community, a facilitator for JourneyMates, and a mentor for the New City Fellows Program. She lives with her husband, John, and two sons in Raleigh, NC. She enjoys visiting her daughters at their universities, long walks with friends, and the delights of a good book.